Jackie Reardon
Hans Dekkers

MINDSET
IN DAILY LIFE
CHASING THE MOSQUITOES AWAY

MINDSET PUBLISHERS

for Ellen Baarslag and Sandra Polderman

This book is published by
Mindset Publishers
IJsbaanpad 43
1076 CV Amsterdam
The Netherlands

Translator Beverley Jackson – jacksonacademic.nl
Graphic design Aart Jan Bergshoeff – aartjan.nl
Drawing mosquitoes and stars Merel Barends
Cover designed by Friendly Eyes, Amsterdam

ISBN 978-90-814928-9-8

First edition 2013
Second edition 2015
Third edition 2016
Fouth edition 2018

© 2013/2015/2016 /2018 Mindset Publishers, Amsterdam
Text © 2013/2015/2016/2018 Jackie Reardon and Hans Dekkers

Photo credits
Acceptance: © Tetra Images/Corbis
Good mistakes: © Fotolia
The bird: © Dreamstime
Medusa: © Nikki Evans
Surfguru: iStockphoto – Ant Creations

Mindset ™ is a protected brand in the Benelux – friendlyeyes.com

INDEX

Action is about living fully.
Inaction is the way that we deny life.
– DON MIGUEL RUIZ: The Four Agreements

CHASING THE MOSQUITOES AWAY

THE BEGINNINGS
AND THE METHOD

In 2007 we wrote the book Mindset. Although it was originally intended as a mental guide for sport, we soon discovered that many people were using the Mindset method in different areas of life. People from all sorts of professions, from teachers to health care workers, from business people and lawyers to musicians, told us the book had enriched their lives. This inspired us to write a sequel: a book that is less about sport and more about mindset in everyday life.

The mindset method works in four stages:
1. Making a conscious choice to adopt action thinking instead of story thinking
2. Six pillars for more self-knowledge and better self-management
3. Four types of concentration for attention control
4. Seven instruments for achieving mental tranquillity

Mindset is based on the belief that we have a choice as to how to approach the world and ourselves. We describe a course of life that you may decide to adopt.

– Do you choose to live on the basis of 'story thinking': constantly judging both yourself and the other, distracted, fearful, rushed and impatient? Another characteristic of story thinking is the constant noise in your head - like being attacked by mosquitoes - random thoughts about the past and the future, which do nothing to advance the things you really want to focus on.

– Or do you choose to live on the basis of 'action thinking': observing without judging, focusing your attention on the here and now. Continuously investing by giving all your actions quality. Being relaxed and focused at the same time, calm and present at the same moment? Action thinking is having a clear understanding of the quality of your thoughts and being capable of choosing where to focus your attention. You learn how to chase the mosquitoes away.

To choose to live on the basis of action thinking, and to change your mode of thinking and behaviour, you first need insight.

We combine two approaches that you can use to make action thinking tangible and easy to train. One of these approaches has to do with insight and raising your consciousness of your behaviour by making use of Mindset's six pillars, derived from mindfulness. The other one has to do with controlling your attention and using the four concentrations, derived from the world of sport.

 The pillars structure your self-management, and the concentrations help you to know precisely what you're focusing on. They are the two wings of the bird (see below). If one of them is not working, the bird can't fly.

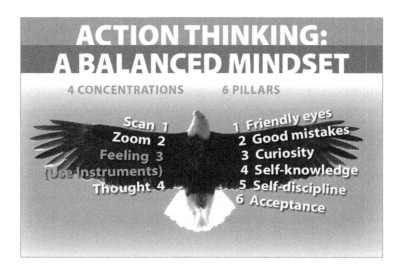

We shall explain each of these six pillars, one step at a time, as well as the four concentrations, and apply them to everyday life.

The first section of the book, on the pillars, provides a philosophical framework for the method and teaches insight into better self-management. The second part, on the different types of concentration, focuses on practical situations in everyday life and offers a program in which you can train your mindset.

Mindset in daily life grew out of our experiences with *Mindset* and consists of further reflections on the subject. No one can achieve his or her best performance in sport without reaching 'feeling', one of the four concentrations. The same applies to people's actions in everyday life. Action starts with feeling. One of the most important goals of this book is to clarify the concept of 'feeling' with practical, concrete examples. 'Feeling' is the essential bridge between thought and action, and practical instruments are needed to gain access to it.

We are convinced that after reading *Mindset in daily life*, 'feeling' will no longer seem like an abstract, vague and rather woolly concept. Both *Mindset* and *Mindset in daily life* were written to provide tools that can help turn impatience, tension and frustration into self-confidence and pleasure. We based many of our insights on the practice of meditation and the philosophy of life that are associated with mindfulness. We gratefully acknowledge the lessons we have learnt from the work of a number of inspiring individuals. In particular, we should like to thank S.N. Goenka, Jon Kabat-Zinn, Joseph Goldstein, Eckhart Tolle, Marshall B. Rosenberg, Stephen Covey and Anthony Robbins.

This book, and the method discussed in it, also derived inspiration from the many books, studies, meditation courses and academic literature on the workings of the conscious mind. For more information about these sources, see the list of recommended literature at the back of the book.

With our method, we try to make all these studies and experiences tangible and to supply ways of putting them into practice, with a view to encouraging a more balanced and effective way of life.

The knowledge itself is by now widely accepted, but it is not widely applied. In other words, everyone knows about it, but few put it into daily practice. Given that action thinking generates so much energy and gives so much pleasure, this is rather peculiar.

Our goal is to present a number of complex theories in a down-to-earth and light-hearted way, thus being able to avoid any surprise attacks by mosquitoes.

We are delighted to be able to offer you a free online mental video program to show you exactly how to deal with the mosquitoes

www.friendlyeyes.com

In the following chapters, we explain the difference between story thinking and action thinking. We shall base these explanations partly on anecdotes and examples that may sound rather familiar. In fact you may be able to have a good laugh at yourself from time to time, when you recognize yourself in one of the situations we describe.

'TO BE OR NOT TO BE'

To be or not to be, that is the question. This line from Shakespeare's *Hamlet* is perhaps the most famous quotation from world literature. The arch-doubter Hamlet ponders to himself whether it is better to live or die: to accept life with all its responsibilities or to be released from them. Hamlet loses himself in thought and has difficulty taking action. He remains a worrier, a brooder, and suffers because of it.

We all have a bit of Hamlet in us. We often find ourselves paralyzed by the noise of constant thinking. Sometimes we turn things over our minds endlessly without taking action, or the action we do take is only half-hearted, held back by doubts. Hamlet's famous words seem to imply a choice, but he is unable to choose. Frequently, we scarcely seem able to take on board the idea that we have a choice, whether or not to act. And we *do* have a choice.

Suppose you have an assignment to write that must be finished within seven days. You have to do it in your own time, after work. You dread having to do it, dread it so much that you turn on the TV straight after dinner and keep zapping, until there is no point in starting on the assignment. It weighs you down, you feel guilty, and that makes you feel even more exhausted. As the deadline approaches, that feeling keeps getting worse and you actually find a sense of panic taking over. You stifle those feelings by watching sports on TV. Then something unexpected happens: your TV breaks down, you're looking at a blank screen. You won't have time to take the set to be repaired until the weekend, and suddenly you have an ocean of time. You sit down at your computer and write the assignment in two evenings. A wonderful feeling. But you're constantly thinking to yourself: why on earth didn't I just turn the TV off before? Next time you have an assignment, you sit down at your computer after dinner instead of turning the TV on. You realize that you really had a very simple choice to make, but that your doubts, insecurity and worries kept you back from making the right decision.

'Mindset' distinguishes between story thinking and action thinking. Two completely opposite approaches to life. Story thinking is characterized by a constant noise in your head, attachment to the past and the future, thoughts that are irrelevant or judgmental. In many cases, you no longer know how to turn these thoughts off.

Action thinking is characterized by non-judgmental observation and being in the here and now, by investing all actions with quality. The most familiar form of action thinking is what is often called 'flow': a state in which time seems to stand still, and all our actions seem to go automatically.

Story thinking is the opposite: our actions seem like a malfunctioning machine. In other words, even our body doesn't function smoothly any more, hampered by an endless flood of thoughts. Everything we do seems difficult and hard work, because we're linking our actions to the past and future instead of being present in the moment. Again and again, we allow ourselves to be distracted by a million things that are simply not relevant.

Action thinking means being able to relax and focus at the same time. You become aware of distractions and are capable of directing your attention and choosing exactly what you want to focus on. You're present in the moment.

We can choose to adopt the enhanced attention of action thinking (to be) and to reject the paralysis of story thinking (not to be). Only then can we make good use of our potential. The Mindset method provides simple tools or instruments that can help to neutralize disruptive thoughts whenever they occur and to focus completely on what we're doing. Hamlet illustrates an extreme case of story thinking. We don't have to be pale replicas of Shakespeare's tragic hero. If we take action, we can leave the hesitant and unhappy Hamlet behind us and move on.

IKKYU

Action thinking is really quite simple, and that is precisely the problem! Here is a famous Zen anecdote[1]:

One day a man of the people said to Zen master Ikkyu, 'Master, will you please write for me some maxims of the highest wisdom?'

Ikkyu immediately took his brush and wrote the word: 'Attention.'

'Is that all?' asked the man. 'Will you not add something more?'

Ikkyu then wrote twice running: 'Attention. Attention.'

'Well,' remarked the man rather irritably, 'I really don't see much depth or subtlety in what you have just written.'

Then Ikkyu wrote the same word three times running: 'Attention. Attention. Attention.'

Half-angered, the man demanded, 'What does that word 'attention' mean anyway?'

Ikkyu answered gently, 'Attention means attention.'

This story describes action thinking perfectly. It is not just what Ikkyu says, but also how he says it, that shows the meaning of action thinking. We often try to resolve our problems or the choices we face by reasoning endlessly, and we lose ourselves in a huge tangle of arguments and doubts. Just like Hamlet. We forget to focus our attention, constructively, on what has to be done in the here and now. To escape from this crippling state and to use our attention and concentration in the best possible way, we need to shift into action thinking. This book is about how to do it.

1 Philip Kapleau ed.: *The Three Pillars of Zen: Teaching, Practice, and Enlightenment*. Anchor Books Editions, New York, 2000.

THE STAR AND THE CLOUD
OF MOSQUITOES

Action thinking is a star shining in the sky, story thinking is a cloud of mosquitoes buzzing around our head. Since the star seems far away, we think we could never manage to bathe in its light. Unconsciously we may even be afraid of how good things might be if we were to live differently. After all, old patterns simply feel more familiar. 'The best I can hope for is...', 'You know how it is...', 'I'm just not cut out for that...' 'But that's how I always do things, a leopard can't change his spots...'. Sometimes we don't seem to want to admit that we would be much better off if we changed our mindset. Just as we seldom allow ourselves to experience silence, and think that every pause has to be filled up with chatter or unrealistic daydreaming. That cloud of buzzing mosquitoes appears much closer to us than the distant light from the star. It seems more familiar, and so we think it's 'normal'. Actually, it's not normal at all. The light radiated by the star, action thinking, is really within reach. And switching to action thinking is much simpler than we may think. Obviously, every person has a bright side and a darker, more shadowy side. The shadowy side will never vanish altogether. Probably we would not even want it to, if we want to remain 'human' instead of changing into a luminous angel or sugar-sweet fairy. Or a pure man or woman of action, who never indulges in lazy daydreams and who acts and reacts like a robot. Our goal is to bend the shadowy side that troubles us as much as possible towards the light. So that we don't get bogged down in a rut, in despondency, fatigue or indecisiveness, and become 'malfunctioning machines'.

Let's put some examples of the two mindsets between which we can choose next to each other and look at the differences.

Story thinking	Action thinking
past/present	here and now
judgment	observation
rationalizing	visualizing
absent	alert
noise	silence
holding on	letting go
consuming	investing

The point is to gradually bend the qualities or elements in the left-hand column, one step at a time, towards those in the right-hand column. These contrasts are obviously relative, not absolute. The attributes in the left-hand column don't have to be banished altogether, what matters is that you gain insight into your patterns of behaviour. The qualities or elements in the right-hand column need space to grow.

Past/present versus here and now

You're on holiday in Bangkok. Last year you were in Hawaii and next year you want to go to Sydney. While you're walking down the

Khao San Road you take a lot of photos to look at later during dinner. Whilst taking the photos, you're constantly talking to your partner about how beautiful Hawaii was and how excited you are about the prospect of going to Sydney next year. You hardly pay any attention to where you actually are. *Alternatively*, you walk down the Khao San Road and allow yourself to be flooded with all the impressions and asian sensations. You enjoy the moment.

Judgment versus observation

A meeting. You think that your colleague doesn't understand the issue and has too little background information. Silently you judge her, stop listening, and withdraw into your shell in irritation. *Alternatively*, you try to listen attentively to her point of view, without judging and without immediately interrupting. You ask open questions and only formulate your own position after listening to the answers.

Rationalizing versus visualizing

You have a job interview next week. The rationalizing approach will involve weighing up all the pros and cons of applying for the job. That will dampen your enthusiasm and you will dread the interview. You get stuck in rationalizations and they give you an oppressive feeling. *Alternatively*, you could adopt a visualizing approach, in which you imagine yourself going to the interview. You feel relaxed and strong. You see the interview in your mind's eye and it goes well.

Absent versus alert

If you don't concentrate when mending an item of clothing or cooking a meal because your thoughts are elsewhere, you will prick your finger or throw the wrong ingredient in the pan. Your observation will be poor because you are too engrossed in thoughts. *Alternatively*, you could invest all your visual and physical attention to your actions. Then these things won't happen; your actions will acquire quality because you are alert, in the here and now.

Noise versus silence

You are stuck with a problem that you find impossible to solve. It carries on rattling through your head. There is a pent-up sense of frustration. *Alternatively* you could decide to take ten minutes off, ten minutes in which you stop looking for a solution. You leave the building, go for a walk, and allow your thoughts to calm down. You experience silence.

Holding on versus letting go

While putting the luggage in the car, you're afraid that your partner will do it the wrong order, which would make it very difficult to get to certain things. You keep checking everything. *Alternatively*, you can decide to trust him, because you realize how unimportant it is.

Consuming versus investing

After attending the first lesson in a French course, you can't formulate a single good sentence in French when you meet up with your French girlfriend. Irritated, you switch back to English. *Alternatively*, you could decide that it doesn't really matter that your french isn't flawless. With healthy self-mockery you continue in your pigeon french. Both you and your girlfriend have a good laugh at your struggle to piece the words together.

It is strange that we're often inclined to hold onto the kinds of behaviour listed in the left-hand column. In some way or other, they seem more familiar. 'That's the way we've always done it' or 'It just feels more comfotable'. Altering this behaviour feels awkward, uncomfortable. Why is it, that we seem to be addicted to the buzzing mosquitoes of story thinking, that never leave us alone, and find it so hard to focus on the star of action thinking?

Perhaps the answer to this question lies in certain reflections on the ego. The ego is a mental construction from which we believe that we derive our identity. It's made up completely of past and future: the personal history we have built up, the expectations we cherish, and our aspirations for the future. In the course of our lives, we build up views, opinions and judgements about others and about ourselves, and from that chaotic whole we fashion as consistently as possible an image that we call our identity. The ego can only exist by virtue of being different from other egos.

Standing out from other egos is precisely what gives the ego its *raison d'être*: it lives on clarifying the differences and is constantly busy setting and defining boundaries.

The ego thrives on story thinking. You might say that ego and story thinking are two sides of the same coin. Since the ego's greatest enemy is the here and now, and since the ego has completely abandoned itself to the past and the future, ego and action thinking are incompatible.

The ego's most characteristic quality is that it does its best to constantly make itself bigger and will fight back whenever any attempt is made to 'suppress it'. The ego thrives on judgments. Judgments disappear with action thinking, which is guided not by judgment but by observation. Every intervention from the ego disrupts that perfect blending of action and consciousness. There is no place for the ego in action thinking. Of course, you don't need to become completely immune to the buzzing cloud of mosquitoes, and your ego will never disappear altogether. But once you've learned to recognize the story thinker sooner, you'll find it easier to deal with the ego and to create more balance in your life.

Let's take another look at why we are so attached to the buzzing cloud of mosquitoes. Strangely enough, it's precisely because it irritates and stings us! Our ego likes to be attacked and to be constantly fending off difficult onslaughts from the outside: these attacks confirm the ego's difference from other people, and it is from that contrast that the ego derives its identity and *raison d'être*. For the ego, it is inconceivable that he is much the same as other people.

Don't you know someone like that from your surroundings: that person with the huge ego? Someone who will almost die without someone to argue with. It's having arguments that enables him to constantly parade his image. His ego is a drum and a trumpet at the same time. The mosquitoes make a cacophony of noise. The person grows and grows. But he doesn't see that his growth consists of lumps... We can probably also find that ego in ourselves. Everyone sometimes has a tendency to be defensive and 'parade his image' at someone else's expense. The cloud of mosquitoes obscures the star and we are too afraid or proud to chase them away.

The task we need to take on, then, is not to see the ego-drummer, whether in someone else or in ourselves, as an irritating windbag. The Vipassana meditation teacher S.N. Goenka has a wonderful discussion of this subject. In his view, we should adopt a friendly manner to someone who polishes his ego in this way, and treat him as a 'kind, ignorant person'. If we fall back on story thinking in relation to the person, it only makes matters worse. We would only be adding more 'contamination' to the atmosphere and achieve the reverse of what we might wish. Malice and hatred never change anything for the better. Compassion can do so.

To approach a big ego with its own resources will actually strengthen the ego and make it grow even bigger. These resources will actually pump it up. Compassion and kindness will soften the drummer's ego, since these offer little to feed on (argument and aggression). If approached like that, the ego is more likely to become deflated, like a balloon.

We advise you to look at yourself in this way when you know that you have made a huge fuss (cacophony) about nothing. After all, you yourself may be a 'kind, ignorant person'.

ACTION
Describe a situation in which the story thinker (ego-drummer) in yourself asserted himself or herself. What would you now do differently?

A FOOTSTEP ON THE MOON

When Neil Armstrong became the first man to set foot on the moon, he spoke the immortal words: 'That's one small step for a man, one giant leap for mankind.' What we often ignore is the fact that that one footstep came at the end of a gigantic operation, an enterprise that filled it with historic significance. To make that giant leap possible, countless efforts had been made, countless 'small steps'.

It's not only the noise in our heads that belongs to the story thinking that weighs us down and paralyzes us. Another part of story thinking may be setting a very high, ambitious goal, a goal that is unrealistic or that you expect to achieve far too quickly. It is only by making changes with great precision, one step at a time, and by setting clear, realistic goals, that real progress can be made. This approach will also confer a sense of satisfaction in the chosen path. A word of caution, however: if one of your thoughts is 'once I've reached this goal I'll be happy', we would see that as a sign of ignorance. For there's only one moment at which you can be happy, and that is right now. Of course you can feel really satisfied and look back on all your hard work when you achieve something, but if you don't enjoy the process itself, you're selling yourself short. In the most extreme case, this can lead to burnout.

People generally suffer from burnout if they work hard without deriving any pleasure from it.

We often read in the media that success is there for the taking and is easy to reach. All you need to do is to sign on for one of the millions of talent shows and by next year you'll be famous. Successful people who inhabit a glamorous world fire our imagination, and reports in the media make us believe that there's something missing in our own lives. It's as if everyone should be able to make a smash hit in the wink of an eye. The realization that we must pay attention to numerous essential 'little things' seems to be getting lost. And anyway, what is that 'big thing' we're aiming for? Will it really make us so much happier and more contented, once we've got there? Or are we condemning ourselves to an endless life of story thinking, because we cannot stop believing that we will only be happy once we have achieved that 'big thing'?

It's important to guard against constantly shifting into the role of consumer: assuming that there is a quick fix for every problem, every desire. Patience is in short supply. Sometimes we may think the odds are stacked against us, a feeling that leads to bitterness, which is expressed in apathy, envy and/or jealousy. But it is in fact the small steps we take, and take patiently, that bring real satisfaction. They can banish the frustrated sense of banging into brick walls. Why? Because this approach helps us to focus on the now. Every step we take requires an effort and is valuable, because it brings us closer to our goal, and that knowledge alone gives satisfaction. But the goal will never be our final destination, since the satisfaction comes from taking each footstep.

MEDUSA'S SPELL

One of the best-known tales from Greek mythology is about Medusa. She is found in a compromising position with Poseidon, in a temple dedicated to the goddess Athene. In a rage, Athene decides to change Medusa's hair into serpents. She also ensures that anyone who gazes at Medusa's face, which is as beautiful as it is terrifying, will turn to stone. Medusa can say goodbye to Poseidon...

It sometimes seems that we too have looked at Medusa. In what respect? We often slouch in front of the TV or stare at the computer screen or our mobile phone, as if the screen has the same effect as Medusa's face. We seem to have turned into stone. We can say goodbye to Poseidon...

Our mobile phones and TV remote controls seem to have become part of our arm. Zapping, looking at messages, surfing the Internet, clicking and downloading all sorts of apps: it all seems to happen without any choice. It's become mechanical, automatic, devoid of choice. Go to a fantastic pop concert, and you'll see people who are constantly checking their e-mail, texting, twittering, whatsapping or facebooking, and meanwhile they're scarcely paying any attention to the music. This behaviour is caused by an amorphous flood of external thoughts and impulses. We succumb to it without any exercise of the will. It's the chaos and noise of story thinking, because it's not based on choice.

Countless different stimuli all around us seem to have taken hold of us, paralyzing us. Like those who have gazed at Medusa, we also have turned into stone.

Action thinking means escaping from the cloud of mosquitoes and breaking through the deadening impulses. By making choices and decisions. Medusa's spell can be broken by simply deciding where and how long you want to devote your attention to something.

ACTIONS against MEDUSA'S SPELL
Choose one or more of the following actions:
'I'm not taking my mobile with me when I go to a concert.'
'I'm going to check my mail three times a day.'
'If I'm talking to someone else, I'll leave my mobile in my bag.'
'Before picking up the remote control, I'll decide what program I want to watch by looking through the guide.'
'I will spend maximum 10 minutes a day on Facebook.'
'I will spend maximum three times, three minutes a day twittering.'

THE COOK AND
THE TEN MOSQUITOES

Action thinking is based on brief, vigorous thoughts that are linked to clear decisions and statements. Story thinking is full of endless discussions, complaints, comparisons and doubts about irrelevant things. As we've already said, story thinking often seems much easier, and sometimes we even find it entertaining. Compared to story thinking, the products of action thinking often seem rather meagre and boring. They're sometimes even classified as 'politically incorrect', as if you were blowing your own trumpet. If we formulate clearly and concisely what we want, we may be thought arrogant or greedy. It appears that we're very concerned what other people think of us, and hide behind a façade of modesty. Let's look at a few examples. Someone has cooked a perfect meal, in which the chicken has turned out absolutely delicious. Someone compliments the cook: 'Fantastic chicken, one of the best dishes I've ever had!' The story-thinking cook might react:

1. 'Yes, but I think the chicken was a bit dry';
2. 'Actually this chicken worked out better last time';
3. 'I can't believe it worked out so well';
4. 'Last week I had some of Marie's, and hers was really perfect';
5. 'Yes, it's because I've got a new oven';

6. 'It's just a recipe, you know, I'm not the sort of cook that can just put a meal together by instinct. I'm hopeless at improvising';
7. 'I could have used more herbs, to make it a bit tastier';
8. 'Now I've proved that I really do cook better than my wife';
9. 'Do you think so? Well, it's just chicken, nothing special';
10. 'Actually I've got another chicken recipe that is even more delicious'.

These are ten mosquitoes of story thinking. Some of these reactions to the compliment probably sound very familiar. We can learn to convert these automatic disclaimers into reactions reflecting action thinking.

1. Silence, and a warm look of appreciation.
2. Saying 'Thank you'.

It's important that you adopt the kind of action thinking that goes with you. It may seem very simple, but in everyday life it's often difficult to find the right words. We have the constant feeling that we ought to say more, but it's usually unnecessary.

The next few chapters deal with the six pillars. These are not the pillars of the Greek temple in which Medusa had such a good time with Poseidon. You can see these pillars as a kind of manual. Because if you apply them every day, you will be doing everything in your power to live a balanced, effective life. This will change feelings of dissatisfaction, impatience, tension and frustration into self-confidence and enjoyment. These pillars sometimes overlap and enhance each other.

THE PILLARS

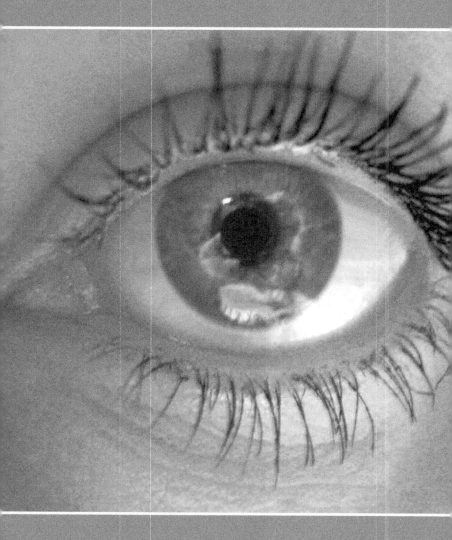

Friendly eyes
'Friendly eyes' create safety

FRIENDLY EYES

FRIENDLINESS, ENERGY, OR MUST IT BE A NOBEL PRIZE?

The first pillar and the foundation of action thinking is 'friendly eyes'. By 'friendly eyes' we mean a state of mind. If you look objectively, and non-judgmentally, both at yourself and at the outside world, you will no longer be at the mercy of your emotions. When something is not going well, either with yourself or with someone else, try not to react immediately with some kind of judgment. It may sound a bit soft, 'friendly eyes', but our experience with Mindset training has shown how important this pillar is, how powerfully it can work and even generate energy. Instead of looking with 'unfriendly eyes' (looking judgmentally, with anger, irritation, or impatience) you can change your state of mind – simply by looking differently – into one of friendliness and patience. Besides saving a lot of energy, this will also elicit more pleasant reactions from other people.

It will introduce a sense of security and calm into situations, not just for yourself but also for those around you. This will help to dispel the constant dependence on approval or disapproval. It is sometimes suggested that using friendly eyes may construct a sort of shield or armour of indifference. This might indeed be true, if you didn't combine it with the third and fourth pillars, curiosity and self-knowledge. The pillars are all inextricably interconnected.

By practising looking at your own and other people's actions with friendly eyes, sportspeople can develop a far more balanced kind of behaviour and ultimately achieve more. How often do you see world-class sports competitors losing their temper, swearing, grumbling, or complaining out loud? Very seldom, and almost always very briefly. The best sports competitors are very well aware that 'unfriendly eyes' have the potential for ruining their concentration and achievements.

Let's get back to the cook and his ten mosquitoes. In response to a compliment about his delicious chicken dish, he could also graciously accept the compliment and be pleased with what he has achieved, as we describe in his reaction as an action thinker. That's what we call 'looking at yourself with friendly eyes'. And even if, for instance, the dish is not quite so good as on some other occasion or with some other recipe, this still need not cause him to judge himself negatively.

So what are the benefits of 'friendly eyes' for yourself?

1. You'll feel better about your cooking abilities and yourself.
2. You'll feel more inclined to make the same dish again (and possibly to try out some minor improvements).
3. You'll have a more objective view instead of expressing all kinds of reasons to play down what you achieved.

What are the benefits of 'friendly eyes' for others?

1. They will feel more secure in your company.
2. They will dare to open up to you more.
3. They will not hide behind any shield or armour; all subjects will in principle be open to discussion.

Looking with friendly eyes is made difficult by the dominant role of judgmental attitudes in our society. In TV talk shows, in newspapers, blogs and magazines, in gossip at work or in the family, we are constantly confronted with black-and-white judgments. It often starts when we are very young. As soon as the visitors go home, everyone starts talking about them. We are brought up to form judgments all the time. Gossip is addictive, because it feeds our egos. Instead of looking at yourself and the world around you with a judgmental attitude, you could try just observing. Without immediately forming judgments, you could try to watch and observe as objectively as possible. It makes you less vulnerable because you don't take everything personally. It saves a lot of mental energy and induces a calm frame of mind. The other person will feel a greater sense of security in your company.

Friendly eyes does not mean glossing over your mistakes and mindlessly accepting whatever you hear. It means being able to recognize your emotions at the right time and anticipating them, before they have a chance to unbalance you and draw you into story thinking. This helps you conserve the energy you need to focus on the things that matter and to keep the cloud of mosquitoes at bay.

Training action thinking means, among other things, training a curious, friendly and non-judgmental kind of attention. In psychology too, more and more research is being conducted on the effect of this attitude, which is also referred to as mindfulness. This attitude has a positive impact on our everyday feelings of well-being, and on our experiences of pain and stress.

It's not only the habit of constantly making judgments that gets in our way when we try to train the pillar of 'friendly eyes'. Being too fixated on results will also prevent us from performing tasks in a balanced way, and with satisfaction. 'My only goal is to win this match.' That's one of the things you'll hear most often from people involved in sport at every level. You could easily find analogies with wanting to be better than your colleagues, to achieve a particular promotion, to get a bigger car or the latest iPad, and so on. Were Mother Teresa, Nelson Mandela, F.W. de Klerk and Albert Einstein worrying about winning a Nobel Prize, or were they focusing on what matters, working on the basis of friendly eyes and effective energy? The strange thing about 'wanting to win' is that it actually has no content at all. Wanting to win and being fixated on the result takes you away from the here and now and disturbs your concentration. What is more, winning in itself doesn't serve any purpose, it doesn't set you firmly on the road towards what you want to achieve, but simply creates more tension. This in turn will lead you to fall back on story thinking. The mosquitoes will be coming at you and biting you from all sides. Action thinking is investing your actions with quality, and improving one step at a time by taking action. Only then can you really win: from yourself. Setting yourself an achievable, modest goal and pursuing it as well as possible will give you daily satisfaction and feel like 'winning', provided you do so with the benefit of friendly eyes.

Why do we use the expression 'friendly eyes', when we're talking about not being judgmental? Isn't 'friendly' in itself a kind of judgment? In one of his famous lectures, the Zen master Shunryu Suzuki says: 'When I say to see things-as-it-is, what I mean is to practice hard with our desires – not to get rid of desires, but to take them into account.'[1]

In short, it's impossible to become a completely objective machine that only registers what happens. Nor would that be desirable.

There's always a danger that you might change into 'a thing that observes other things', a sort of machine that uses friendly eyes to keep the world out. After all, you could use friendly eyes to ensure that nobody can ever 'get at you' and to stay safely within your comfort zone. Looking at yourself and others with friendly eyes doesn't mean changing into a cold, unemotional observer, and it doesn't mean that you don't care. Applying friendly eyes in the right way will produce an active, open attitude: friendly and energetic, enthusiastic, pleasant, relaxed and patient. Friendly eyes can also lead, if necessary, to a direct and friendly confrontation. From an inner sense of security, you'll have the courage to leave your comfort zone to face challenges, again and again. In other words, it's the beginning of a never-ending personal transformation.

Gratitude

Gratitude is inextricably connected to 'friendly eyes'. This will immediately evoke 'friendly eyes' both for yourself and for the other. If you're ungrateful, the result will generally be the opposite. One of the leading authorities on the subject of 'gratitude', Robert Emmons,[2] has demonstrated in numerous studies that gratitude is one of the best strategies for achieving happiness. Gratitude means being happy with who you are and what you've got: your health, your partner, your family, your friends, your work, your abilities, your children, your house, your pet, music, literature, and so on. It means starting to think about your life with gratitude. Count your blessings. Research has shown that people who have the habit of counting their blessings actually enjoy better health. They are also less depressed, anxious, lonely, envious, and neurotic.[3] A great time for 'practising' that gratitude (since this too is a skill), is during the walk that is described in a separate chapter on 'the art of action'. It's an essential part of it.

1 Shunryu Suzuki: *Branching Streams Flow in the Darkness. Zen Talks on the Sandokai*. University of California Press, Berkeley and Los Angeles, 1999.
2 Emmons, Robert A., & McCullough, Michael E.: 'Counting blessings versus burdens: An experimental investigation of gratitude and subjective well-being in daily life'. *Journal of Personality and Social Psychology*, vol. 84 (2). 2003.
3 Sonja Lyubomirsky: *The How of Happiness*. Penguin Press. New York, 2007.

ACTIONS for FRIENDLY EYES

1. Every day, think of three things for which you were grateful that day.
2. Decide that today, you're going to look at everything around you with friendly eyes. Resolve not to become irritated or angry about anything.

When you're talking to someone, keep running over in your mind whether what you're saying is friendly. Realize that you'll acquire an even greater feeling of security once you've been doing this every day for an extended period of time.

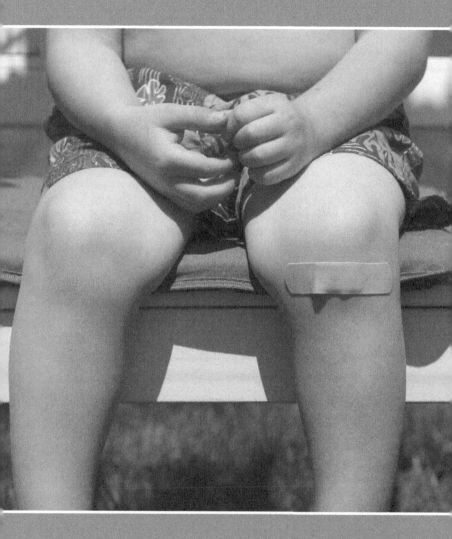

Good mistakes

'Good mistakes' means forgiveness

GOOD MISTAKES

A RED SOCK

Those who don't do anything never make mistakes.
– THÉODORE DE BANVILLE

Three white shirts, a cream-coloured pair of trousers, a white tennis skirt, and some white underwear. That's how it all went into the washing machine. And now it all comes out pink. Because of one stray red sock... How do you react?

We call mistakes 'good mistakes' if the intention was good, when something went wrong or happened by accident. In other words, the mistake was not deliberate. We also use the phrase 'good mistakes' to refer to the significance you attach to an event. How do you react to an event, and what kind of energy do you invest in it? That's why the case of the red sock comes under this heading. Every time something 'goes wrong', you learn from your reaction. You could make your pink washing into a catastrophe and curse yourself. That wasted energy is story thinking. Even the 'mistake' of the red sock can be turned into something positive. You can see the funny side of it. You can take another look at the 'mistake', with friendly eyes:

· How did this mistake happen?
· What can I learn from it?
· How can I prevent this happening in future?
· How quickly can I get over this mistake?

What we mean by a good mistake is a tangible event: something goes 'wrong' through your own actions or those of someone else. What concerns us here is how you react to it.

An example of a good mistake caused by your own actions:
You have a very important meeting with the manager of another company in a hotel that is 50 miles away from where you live. You've never been there before. You look up on a Routeplanner how long it will take to drive there. Not bad, it should be possible to get there in 50 minutes. The night before, you put the location in your GPS, so that you can leave early in the morning. You get up with what feels like plenty of time to spare, and check your e-mail while you're having breakfast with your children. Blast! One of the e-mails reminds you that you've forgotten something. You reply to the mail straight away. You take a quick look at your watch and see that, luckily, you still have an hour to get to your appointment. You jump into your hatchback and let rip.

Twenty minutes later you're swearing to yourself, since a lane is closed and you're stuck in a three-mile tailback. You look in your bag and discover to your great irritation that you've left your mobile phone on the kitchen table. You arrive twenty minutes late, slam the door of your car and almost strangle yourself in your haste, because your scarf gets stuck in the door. You walk in as calmly as possible, and greet the manager with a fake smile on your face. Inside, you're seething. How you look back on this event later will depend on your level of awareness.

Two conclusions are possible

1. You can't believe that you always have so much to think about and that this should have happened to you again. What incredibly bad luck, even though you had prepared it so well.
2. You realize that you should have got up half an hour earlier, as a result of which everything would have gone differently.

You would have had time to pay attention to your children. You could have dealt with your e-mails before or after breakfast. You would have had your mobile phone with you. You could have calmly gone through the mental preparation for the conversation while waiting in the tailback.

You wouldn't have half strangled yourself with your scarf.
Your smile wouldn't have been fake but real.
In short: you would have been alert and relaxed for the meeting.

An example of 'good mistakes' caused by someone else's actions
You've booked a restaurant for 7 p.m., but when you arrive there's no table waiting for you. You'll have to wait for an hour, because someone got the reservation time wrong. Allowing yourself to get angry and ruin the mood for the entire evening obviously doesn't help.

If you look at this second example as a good mistake ('these things happen'), you will forgive the other person and remain in action thinking. Depending on how the waiters react, you decide whether or not you feel like hanging around for an hour. If so, you take pleasure in the surroundings and the company. If not, you go off in search of an alternative with positive energy.

Perhaps these two examples seem very obvious. But don't underestimate how much energy most people waste every day by getting irritated about 'errors' like this and not learning from them.

Another example of good mistakes
You're at the supermarket. The cashier is very slow, you
see someone jumping the queue, the wheels of your trolley
keep getting stuck, the person behind you is standing too
close, and you've forgotten the milk. All these things have
put you in a very bad mood. This makes doing the shopping
an exhausting experience.

The main point about good mistakes is that if you do something
with the 'error' afterwards, there aren't really any errors, only
learning experiences. You realize that everyone is 'doing his best'
in his own way, just like you. Of course, differences in ability,
insight, experience and intelligence mean that doing your best
won't be the same from one person to the next. This gives a whole
new meaning to the notion of 'failure'. As long as you're doing
your best, you can't really fail. Instead, you have an exercise in acceptance, a way of practising 'friendly eyes', a moment of insight
into the fact that there are many more important things to spend
your energy on, and so on. If you're curious (third pillar) about
your own reaction to something that goes wrong, everything appears in a different light. This will lead to more self-knowledge
(fourth pillar) and less irritation.

Once you realize that you can't change the past, forgiveness and
acceptance are the only logical reactions. 'Good mistakes' really

means forgiving yourself or others. Based on that forgiveness, you make new plans. You take action. It's basically very simple: the only way to stop yourself getting stuck in wasteful mental energy (story thinking) is by taking action (action thinking).

It helps to react to an 'error' by using an instrument to switch to action thinking. Take this example. You accidentally deleted a file you had worked on all morning without making a backup. Panic strikes and you're furious at yourself. At a moment like this you can use a specific instrument, such as breathing (we discuss these instruments at length later on). You spend one minute counting your natural breathing; then you lower your rate of breathing to six inhalations and exhalations a minute. As a result you will be more clear-headed, your anger will subside, you'll calm down and be better able to make decisions.

Forgiveness

In the same way that gratitude is linked to friendly eyes, forgiveness is linked to good mistakes. Forgiveness is first and foremost in not being judgmental, not condemning. That applies to forgiving yourself just as much as forgiving other people. Like gratitude and compassion (which is linked to acceptance), forgiveness helps to lower stress. All three will 'soften' your state of mind and help to produce inner calm. Accusing people or feeling guilty can both be resolved by forgiveness. Forgiveness releases energy that would otherwise – if you don't forgive – be directed inwards and gnaw away at you. To be 'eaten up' by this or that emotion is a very apt expression for this. Forgiveness helps you approach other people with more openness. And ultimately helps you develop deeper relationships and friendships. So the next time you notice yourself 'losing it' by getting annoyed at a slow cashier, a queue jumper or whatever, try a bit of self-irony, laugh at it, and forgive yourself for sliding into story thinking. And forgive the other person too. If you don't, you're only harming yourself. The 'good mistakes' approach creates space that enables you to quickly escape from story thinking, releasing energy for curiosity.

ACTION for GOOD MISTAKES

1. Decide today that, if someone does something that annoys you, you forgive the person straight away.
2. Reflect on an unpleasant moment in your life that was caused due to your own behaviour. It still remains an embarrassment to you and it feels like a thorn in your side. Decide once and for all to forgive yourself.
   For example:
   How you spoke to your partner, mother, father or child.
   The bad results you got for an important exam or match, because you hadn't done the necessary work.
   The disappointment you feel about breaking a promise to yourself.
3. Decide to forgive somenone who has caused you unhappiness or sorrow in the past.

Curiosity
Curiosity enables growth

CURIOSITY

THE COCONUT

*The sun shines and warms and lights us and we have no
curiosity to know why this is so; but we ask the reason of
all evil, of pain, and hunger, and mosquitoes
and silly people.*
– RALPH WALDO EMERSON

When we came across this quotation from Emerson, it was a delightful surprise. It sounds rather like our story about the cloud of mosquitoes and the star. The sun in Emerson's quote is the star in 'action thinking' and the part about the mosquitoes is our cloud of mosquitoes of story thinking. And 'silly people' are obviously the people all around us who are ignorant . . . or could they be us?

Our curiosity frequently focuses on the silly or negative sides of our behaviour and that of other people. We are far less inclined to focus on things that are important and constructive; we simply tend to forget them or take them for granted, because of the constant buzz of story thinking. For instance, not many people would dare to ask a good friend or colleague to define their best talents or qualities. Constructive criticism is obviously indispensable, but asking about what we're good at can also help us move forward. Appreciation doesn't necessarily lead to complacency or self-satisfaction, it can help to encourage us to pursue a particular path and to carry on developing our strong qualities. Curiosity – provided it's used properly and first and foremost in relation to yourself – is extremely helpful and constitutes the third pillar of action thinking. It provides new insights about yourself and the world around you, making growth and change possible. If you're not curious about yourself, everything will remain as it was, or changes will only take place as a result of ignorance or external influences, things over which you don't have much hold and that will often be of little benefit to you. Without curiosity, changes will take place without your active involvement. That is surely not what you want.

Curiosity is key to personal growth. Changing story thinking into action thinking doesn't mean switching off thinking altogether, it means using new patterns to neutralize the 'noise' of story thinking and to stop identifying with it. Once we realize that a thought, any thought, is just a spark of electricity, it becomes much easier to realize that we ourselves determine whether or not to attach any value to it. The mosquitoes will continue to buzz, but you can learn to move the noise into the background.

A well-known, unpleasant story is told about the way in which hunters catch monkeys in India. They make a hole in a coconut just large enough for a monkey's hand. They put a banana inside the hollowed-out coconut. The coconut is attached to a tree. Once the monkey has got hold of the banana, he won't let it go, and can easily be caught while he is struggling with it.

This is a good metaphor for the lack of curiosity. You've found something you were looking for and hold on tight. A goal is never a final destination, for then curiosity would stop. It seems as if you've reached your goal, but it's precisely holding onto it that stops you moving forward. It's necessary to constantly adopt an open and flexible attitude. This means constantly evaluating your situation and continuing to search for solutions if that situation is no longer satisfactory. That prevents you from stagnating. Action arises from curiosity. At first, that might seem exhausting and impossible to sustain. But as you acquire more insight, you realize that it's not exhausting at all, it's simply a way of actively engaging with life.

Curiosity will help you notice whenever you lapse into story thinking. Together with adopting the 'friendly eyes' and 'good mistakes' approaches, you will learn to recognize patterns that keep repeating themselves. In applying the first two pillars, you will feel safe enough to reflect on your own behaviour. The sooner and more frequently you recognize patterns, the easier it becomes to switch to action thinking, and the less painful it gets to see that you don't always tackle things in the best way. You can even see the funny side, not be ashamed of yourself, and be pleased about the new discoveries you've made. In general, we're not inclined to make changes, because fixed patterns feel comfortable, and because we believe that changing patterns takes energy and effort and may sometimes be painful. That's only a perception (from story thinking), since it actually provides insight and satisfaction to break out of your usual rut and leave your comfort zone. It's outside your comfort zone that you will find creativity, renewal, and magic.

The point is to learn to realize that you can choose, and that you can take action straight away. Not taking action is in fact a sort of 'not-living' or just keeping your life ticking over. It's only by taking action that you express who you are. It's true, as we've said, that the awareness that you have this choice, 'to be or not to be', may feel like a burden and a great responsibility. But you can also see it as exciting. If you look on these choices as a kind of adventure and you don't mind sometimes – or even quite often – 'failing', you'll be able to change your mindset much more quickly. In our philosophy, there's no such thing as failure, as long as you're doing your best and as long as, when things go 'wrong', you think about what you might do differently and take some new action. Try taking the kind of action that feels unfamiliar, this is what we mean by moving 'out of your comfort zone'. Be aware that even when things seem to be 'going wrong', it certainly doesn't mean that you're not doing your best. It also doesn't mean that you're unsuccessful, since from this perspective, you've already succeeded by making an effort.

Of course, it's possible to express curiosity without being really interested. For instance, you might ask someone else's opinion just so that you can say what you think yourself. But that's just pretending to be curious, when what you really want is to express your own opinion without really listening to the other person.

Try not to deny the existence of the cloud of mosquitoes that will frequently be buzzing all around you. Don't be afraid of them, just observe them without judging. Don't identify with them, the mosquitoes are not part of yourself and they're more likely to disappear if you don't start swatting at them.

ACTIONS for CURIOSITY

Decide to take some action that's *outside your comfort zone.*

1. What could you ask one of your best friends in order to get to know him or her better? Instead of falling silent, changing the subject or making the usual jokes about things you actually find difficult to talk about.
2. Go up to a colleague who you normally hardly ever speak to. Ask him or her, for instance: 'I'm working on this or that project, how would you tackle it?'
3. Start a friendly discussion with someone you've never met before, for instance while queuing up for the cashier at the supermarket or in public transport.

It often seems as if there's never a suitable moment to take action like this, but when *would* a moment be suitable? Do we refrain from being curious and allow such moments to slip away, or do we take action, in order to grow?

Self-knowledge
Self-knowledge is shared knowledge

SELF-KNOWLEDGE

TO UZBEKISTAN

The fourth pillar, 'self-knowledge', also essentially involves a simple choice: are you going to avoid looking at your own behaviour (the way you use your voice, your body language, your choice of words, the kind of action you take) because it's too confrontational? Or do you take a good look at how you behave and talk because it's worthwhile? The pillars of curiosity and self-knowledge are closely connected. Without curiosity, you can't achieve self-knowledge.

Suppose you choose the first approach, the one that goes with story thinking. If things go wrong, you decide it's not your own fault, the outside world is to blame. In psychology this is called 'externalizing'. You don't even need to know precisely what the outside world can be blamed for, although externalizing is usually accompanied by detailed arguments and complex lines of reasoning. On the other hand, you might choose action thinking, which is based on taking responsibility, accepting that the decisions we make determine our lives. More importantly: the way in which we decide to react to events determines quite literally our position in life. That is something we think about too little or hardly at all. You can't influence what has already happened, but you can influence the significance you attach to it.

Self-knowledge is a precondition for making conscious change that is really productive. And often if it's productive for you then it will have a positive influence on the people around you. It is also essential for setting goals, since you need to know what is within your powers, and what your abilities are. Self-knowledge may come from introspection, but it's equally important to ask for open and honest feedback from other people, such as your partner, colleagues, friends or coach. Self-knowledge depends on shared knowledge. If you fail to call on other people's help when you're striving to attain self-knowledge, you run the risk of acquiring a skewed, unrealistic self-image. It's obviously of key importance who you take into confidence and ask for their advice. In the following table it shows what you can expect from a story thinker and what you can expect from an action thinker.

Story thinker	Action thinker
Fills in/ego 'I have that too, last week I was with...'	Attentive/quiet neutral body language, friendly eyes
Gossip 'Yes, I know X and Y do this and that...'	Understanding 'I can imagine that must've been a struggle'
Aggressive 'Yeah, well, but why did you do it like that anyway?'	Calm 'Help me to understand what you did/said'
Rushed 'Yes yes, I get it!'	Patient 'Is there anything else you want to say about it?'

It would be good to add a few remarks about self-knowledge and ego here. The ego doesn't like looking at itself, but prefers looking at other people's failings and the causes ('luck') of other people's success. The latter often springs from envy and not from the inspiration that you might derive from other people's success on your own path to personal development. The ego only wants to see itself reaffirmed and doesn't want to change. The ego defends itself, withdraws, attacks, or desires. It only wants to encounter opposition/resistance since that enables it to reaffirm itself.

The 'you too!' form of argument is a typical ego reaction. This refers to the kind of response in which someone always counters criticism by saying that the other person does the same thing:

'Why do you immediately have to start getting aggressive again?'
'Excuse me? As if you can't be aggressive!'
or:
'I think you could have been a bit more lenient with your secretary, about that bit of miscommunication with the board.'
'And I suppose you think that you are the mildest, subtlest person in the world!'

Wouldn't these exchanges have been far more satisfying if the reaction had been curious, seeking to gain self-knowledge. For instance:
'Am I sounding aggressive? I didn't realize. I'm sorry that's how it came across. I simply want to know what you think.'
or:
'You may be right. How would you have dealt with it?'

Silence and compassion

Being open to new things also means creating or allowing gaps in the conversation, moments of silence. For instance by not always reacting straight away to what someone is saying, but by really listening. By not filling in the other person's words, but really trying to understand what the other person is trying to say.

You can listen with friendly eyes and compassion – in what you might call a friendly way:

'I never thought of it like that. Could you explain a bit more what you mean?'

The quest for self-knowledge is about investment, not consumption. Acquired knowledge has to be applied, tried out, trained.

Let's go back to the image of the malfunctioning machine. If you see your behaviour as a malfunctioning machine, you assume that the machine ought to be working properly and that some technician ought to sort it out. You ask someone for advice and carry out all his or her recommendations to the letter. But then, if the machine is still not working properly, you feel you can blame it on the bad or second-rate advice you were given. You go back to get a different, better set of recommendations. In some cases this is passive, consumer-type behaviour, in which you put yourself in the position of dependency. It's important to remain flexible and to adopt an independent attitude. Circumstances, you yourself and other people are constantly changing, which means you have to remain alert. It may take a long time for you to achieve the desired result. Miracle cures and quick fixes are few and far between. You could also see perseverance as being curious for self-knowledge, even though it doesn't produce immediate results. You enjoy the fact that you're constantly moving and have opportunities to ask for advice. With investment-type behaviour, you always take responsibility yourself. You test recommendations and make an effort to explore the way they affect your behaviour and your situation.

Sometimes it seems easier to play down your own behaviour or even to run it into the ground instead of asking advice or evaluating your behaviour in an open exchange of views. Ironically, playing down your own behaviour is precisely the sort of thing that will drain your energy in the long term.

You can be open to, and learn from, the opinions of experienced and sensible people, but in the end it's you who will determine what you want. Let's look at a rather comical example of the kind of conversation we have all probably had at some point.

Compare the following conversations

A is surfing the internet looking at different kinds of holiday packages and hotels in Italy. B is reading the paper.

A: 'Don't you think it's time to plan our holiday?'

B: 'As if the last one was such a success.'

A: 'Oh, so you don't want to go on holiday at all?'

B: 'Of course I do. Still, I hate planning everything in advance.'

A: 'Why?'

B: 'Because then it's all such a disappointment once you get there.'

A: 'How about Italy?'

B: 'All that garlic every day, and the people constantly shouting. And they drive like maniacs.'

A: 'I think June would be a good time.'

B: 'I don't know if I can take any time off in June. There's a load of new projects in the pipeline.'

A: 'Have a look at this website. It looks great in Tuscany.'

A passes B the laptop, but B doesn't want to look at it.

B: 'I hate surfing the internet for holidays. They give you the impression that everything is fantastic and completely unmissable. All a load of nonsense of course.'

A: 'Have you got a better why of preparing for our holiday?'

B: 'In any case not one that comes from a website. And anyway I'm not particularly keen on Italy.'

A: 'There are thousands of websites about every country, you know!'

B: 'I think you'll find there are more websites about holidays in Tuscany alone, than about, say, Uzbekistan.'

A: 'OK, so let's go to Uzbekistan then!'

B: 'Don't be ridiculous. You know perfectly well that's not what I mean.'

A: 'So what do you want?'

B: 'I just don't want to talk about it right now. It makes me feel on edge. Why do we have to talk about holidays now, when it's only February? It turns me off the whole idea.'

A: 'OK fine, then we won't go on holiday this year.'

B: 'That's not what I said at all.

Although this example may seem a little exaggerated, we all know that we occasionally 'can't help' getting into a conversation like this. Even an action thinker will occasionally give into making some silly remark. You may not stay in story thinking as long as in the above exchange, but frustration may often make itself felt, in your answers, your voice, and your body language. We're often unconscious of how incompetently we communicate. There's a lack of self-knowledge and we fail to realize that our conversations are often dominated by story thinking.

Suppose B were to become an action thinker by developing self-knowledge. He would then be more conscious of how he is reacting to A and a completely different conversation would take place: one between two action thinkers.

A is surfing the internet looking at different kinds of holiday packages and hotels in Italy. B is reading the paper.

A: 'Don't you think it's time to plan our holiday?'

B : puts the newspaper to one side.

B: 'Planning is half the fun.'

A: 'How about Italy?'

B: 'Great food and opera on every street corner, terrific!'

A: 'I think June would be a good time for us.'

B: 'I'll check whether I can take time off then. There's a load of new projects in the pipeline, but things can always be arranged.'

A: 'Have a look at this website. It looks great. Tuscany.'

A passes B the laptop, who starts leafing through it.

B: 'It makes me want to immediately book a flight and to leave straight away.'

A: 'Wouldn't it be too crowded in June?'

B: 'Don't be daft. You can always find peaceful, obscure little places.'

A: 'So you like the idea of Tuscany?'

B: 'Let's just do it. Tuscany in June. I'll arrange the final dates with the office.'

A: 'Wow, we've never decided as fast as that before. *Andiamo in Toscana, bella!*'

Phases of learning

Let's turn to look at the process of learning about your own abilities. The table shown below is often used for the various stages of learning.

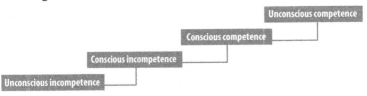

In general, this is what the different stages mean:

Unconscious incompetence (UI): not knowing that you can't do something. You don't realize that you don't have that skill.

Conscious incompetence (CI): knowing that you can't do something. You're aware that you don't have that skill yet.

Conscious competence (CC): being able to do something if you really think about it. If you concentrate really hard, you're usually able to apply that skill.

Unconscious competence (UC): simply being able to do something without thinking about it. You apply the skill instinctively (reflex).

Someone who has a good understanding of this table will deal far more consciously with his own development. He'll constantly be able to go back to the table and apply it to acquire more self-knowledge.

An example of these stages of learning in daily life:
How do you perceive your own computer skills?

Unconscious incompetence: my laptop is really useless, I can't even send e-mails with it.

Conscious incompetence: I can't send e-mails with my laptop yet; I don't know how to install it. I'll get in touch with Jessica, she'll explain exactly how to do it.

Conscious competence: I always have to think hard to remember Jessica's explanation, but I'll figure it out eventually. I even known how to install the other downloads now, not just the e-mail.

Unconscious competence: everything on my computer is working fine.

There are many skills in life that we may not be able to negotiate all that well. We can't even admit it, because we're not aware of it. We don't know that we don't know. The actions that we suggest to acquire self-knowledge, later on, will very probably change that!

Once you have acknowledged problems in your behaviour, you've already taken an important first step in the right direction, from unconscious incompetence to conscious incompetence. It may not always feel so good at first, but that will change. You're on the right path.

Behaviour that can be described as 'unconscious competence' generally feels very good, because you carry out tasks instinctively and effortlessly. Even so, in everyday life it's often useful to know when you are functioning at the stage of 'unconscious competence'. Why? Unconscious competence can lead to communication problems. For instance, a manager with years of experience may be unconscious of the ease with which he solves problems. If he expects his staff to solve them just as quickly, this may cause dissatisfaction and misunderstandings on both sides. The manager is constantly disappointed in the results, and his staff are frightened and frustrated that their work is never good enough or that their efforts are never appreciated. If the manager realized that he operates with unconscious competence and could try to experience his skills on a more conscious level again, he would find it easier to explain how to solve problems.

Instead of thinking that his employees have a lack of discipline, he would understand that it's a lack of knowledge. That would greatly improve the atmosphere, and employees would master the necessary skills faster.

The following actions can speed up the process of finding out certain things about yourself. Asking these questions may take a lot of courage, but the answers may be very illuminating.

ACTION for SELF-KNOWLEDGE

Asks the following people the three questions given below:

a. your partner
b. a colleague
c. a good friend

1. In what area would you say I operate on the level of unconscious competence? Give me an example of what you would say is one of my talents.
2. Do you think I make enough use of this talent? Could you advise me on how to use it more often?
3. In what area do you think I operate on the level of unconscious incompetence? Give an example.

Advice for self-knowledge concerning action number 3

Now that you're aware of what starts off as unconscious incompetence, you can ask the next question to the person who advised you: how do you think I can improve my unconscious incompetence, or would it be more sensible to just accept it and learn to deal with it?

Advice for all actions concerning self-knowledge

Listen to each answer without making judgments, and ask people to clarify what they've said if necessary. NB People are often unwilling to answer questions like this. They don't want to hurt you, they feel uncomfortable, they may even find it hard to think of an answer. If you notice that someone finds it too difficult, just leave it. It's apparently not a good time. You might get the following reaction: 'What do you mean exactly? Could you be a bit more specific?' Our advice is not to go into this too much, since it could limit the scope for an authentic answer. Just say, for instance: 'The point is for you to tell me something that I may not even be conscious of. I think it's exciting to hear what I'm good at. That will help me exploit my strengths better. As far as incompetence is concerned, don't be afraid of hurting me, I can take it! I'd really appreciate your feedback.'

Self-discipline
Self-discipline is joyful anticipation

SELF-DISCIPLINE

EVER HEARD A MILL-HORSE WHISTLING?

Some people regard discipline as a chore.
For me, it is a kind of order that sets me free to fly.
– ACTRESS AND SINGER JULIE ANDREWS

Discipline is joyful anticipation and insight

Discipline is not a millstone hanging round your neck, on the contrary, as Julie Andrew so eloquently suggests, it gives you wings to fly. When you look at it more closely, discipline mainly creates pleasure. Discipline means making time for yourself to do what you've chosen to do. It lays foundations that make creativity possible. It creates a basis from which you can build to your heart's content. Strangely, discipline is often presented in a dreary light, as something that is heavy going, difficult and too much trouble, whereas it's really about gaining insight into what is useful and what gives satisfaction.

Mill-horse or bird?

A mill-horse toils away pulling a heavy burden, going round and round in a treadmill, milling corn. A bird flies around, searching for grains of corn in a cornfield. We have a tendency to associate the horse with discipline and not the bird. That's actually quite sad, since what we associate with 'discipline' has nothing to do with mill-horses and everything to do with birds. Discipline is always related to a goal. The horse doesn't set itself any goals; it's the slave of its owner. It has been made into a machine in the service of producing flour. It has no idea of the goal of all its labours. Ironically, you might say that the mill-horse has actually lost its way. Since discipline serves a goal, it takes on meaning and we can enjoy it. You might see discipline as a kind of joyful anticipation.

Without planning, self-discipline is pointless and empty. Daily reflections on what you want to improve, and on your short-term and long-term goals, will stimulate you to carry on and help to direct your efforts. Being aware of the benefits to be gained from these improvements makes self-discipline enjoyable. This is only possible by linking self-discipline to vision. If you see (visualize) what you want to achieve, making the efforts to achieve it are fun. They spring from creativity and passion. If you don't visualize anything, and simply act without vision or goals, all your actions will be burdensome and you won't achieve anything, even though you're working like a mill-horse.

We want to emphasize that self-discipline is the only real discipline. Real improvement can only be attained if you find the strength for it in yourself. Friendly eyes and good mistakes will help you to achieve this. They provide a sense of security in difficult times, when it's not yet clear that your discipline and insight will lead somewhere. It's not always clear what you're doing it all for. Sometimes you discover that you've taken a wrong path. Don't beat yourself up about it, just start again. Even birds looking for food sometimes search in places with nothing but pebbles. Not giving up, but looking for new approaches: that is discipline too. The fact that you do everything that is within your abilities creates the beginnings of acceptance. Don't allow yourself to get frustrated by a process of trial and error, but accept that it's the only way to progress.

Don't force yourself, don't put yourself under pressure (story thinking), but create the conditions in which you can act effectively and feel a pleasant sense of determination (action thinking). That has to do with your abilities and your knowledge of those abilities. Self-discipline is the opposite of forcing yourself. If you force yourself, it means that you:
1. don't accept your abilities or limitations
2. have too little insight into what you could be concentrating on
3. have too little insight into your own abilities

Insight and joyful anticipation

Putting things off. You know there's a deadline approaching, you know that you frequently put things off until the last minute, you regard this as a 'lack of discipline'. Turn it around, suppose you decide to spend half an hour on the project every day, every morning from 7 to 7.30, you simply get up half an hour earlier. No stress, everything under control, you meet your deadline. Is your habit of putting things off a lack of discipline or a lack of insight? Do you want to keep experiencing stress? Is your ego addicted to it? What is an extra half an hour a day when it gets rid of all the irritability and replaces it with satisfaction and self-respect? Nothing produces more free time than working! That's why discipline equals insight and joyful anticipation.

ACTIONS for SELF-DISCIPLINE

1. Think of a plan that you have been putting off for ages. Decide to take action and to start implementing your plan this week. Be enthusiastic and realize how much fun it is. Decide how, when and what weekly actions you will take until your plan has been achieved.

2. Tidy something up every week that you would normally leave in a mess. It might be your clothes cupboard, your desk or your filing system. These are all things that are actually very easy to arrange and that will give a sense of joyful anticipation.

Acceptance
Acceptance demands courage

ACCEPTANCE

A COMPLETE WASTE OF TIME!

'Acceptance is for losers, people who really don't know what it is to fight.' 'Acceptance: that's just rubbish, totally useless, a complete waste of time. What a load of nonsense, I'm not going to throw in the towel!'
'Why should I accept everything? If I don't like something I say so.' 'Acceptance, that won't get you anywhere. My father never accepted a thing, and he set up a million-dollar company.'

Although these examples are a bit extreme, you do hear people talking about acceptance in these terms. They all reflect the same misunderstanding: real acceptance is quite the opposite of how these critics define it. What we mean by acceptance is not 'throwing in the towel'. On the contrary, it's one of the most challenging, active mental efforts you can make. It takes an enormous effort to look at ourselves, the other person, and the situation we're in, in a non-judgmental way – in other words with friendly eyes – and with acceptance. That's why acceptance is also the most challenging and radical of the pillars. Acceptance demands courage.

Acceptance is the mother of all pillars

'As it is, not as you want it to be': this well-known piece of Oriental wisdom captures the meaning of acceptance perfectly. Don't struggle against the inevitable, don't waste energy attacking that reality, choose to accept the situation as it is and to react to it. In other words, acceptance doesn't mean passivity or resignation or not experiencing anything. On the contrary: acceptance produces so much peace that powerful actions can emerge from it and you can experience everything with heightened attention. Jon Kabat-Zinn, a molecular biologist and researcher who has researched mindfulness and meditation intensively, makes some valuable observations. He says that acceptance offers a way of navigating the ups and downs of our lives. He uses a common analogy, comparing the mind to the surface of an ocean. There are always waves, whether gentle or fierce. There's obviously no point, says Kabat-Zinn, in trying to stop them. He describes a poster showing a yogi with a long white beard and flowing gown riding a surfboard on the waves of a Hawaiian beach. The caption is 'You can't stop the waves, but you can learn to surf.' (Mind/Body Medicine, 1993)

Is acceptance escapism?

Acceptance is opening yourself up to the here and now. Being in the moment may feel pleasant or unpleasant, but by 'opening yourself up' we mean accepting things as they are now. Neither desiring other outcomes or rejecting what is happening. Only then can your actions be pure, without emotions confusing or obscuring them.

This last point is often misunderstood: if you accept everything the way it is, how can you ever change? This is sometimes called the paradox of acceptance. The famous psychologist Carl Rogers based his theory and therapy on this paradox. He said: 'The curious paradox is, when I accept myself just as I am, then I can change.'

Here you see the six pillars all intertwined: friendly eyes giving a sense of security, the 'good mistakes' approach enabling you to see honestly what is not working and to forgive yourself and other people, curiosity helping you define scope for personal growth, self-knowledge helping you identify the qualities you want to develop, and self-discipline in order to persevere and to enjoy what you decide to tackle. If you do all this, the result will be acceptance. But only if you show courage in situations in which you would normally yield or remain silent. It's only from the basis of this acceptance that we can develop in a pleasant way, without constantly punishing ourselves and putting ourselves under pressure. We learn to accept by realizing that we have done everything within our power.

By turning away from the mosquitoes and focusing on the star you will gradually grow into an action thinker. A nice added bonus may be that other people notice the change and become interested in how it works. So indirectly, you would also be helping other people to acquire insight. The mosquitoes gradually fade into the background. All this means that acceptance is only a beginning, not an end in itself.

Take this example:
A policy officer at the local council is 43 years old and has been doing the same job for 15 years. She enjoys her work and does it well. When her manager's job falls vacant, she applies for it. To her surprise, a woman of only 32 gets the job. From that moment onwards, she starts doubting her abilities and enjoys her work far less than before. Her colleagues don't seem to think it strange that a young woman has been appointed to the job, but at the same time she never hears any actual criticism of her own work. Almost every day she has to deal with her sense of frustration, in meetings with the young woman, even when she bumps into her in the corridor. She starts hating her work, and has the idea that her performance is going steadily downhill.

If the policy officer had accepted the new situation, she could not only have prevented the feelings of frustration, but also started on a process of change.

> As soon as the new appointment was announced, the policy officer could have decided to act as follows:
> Congratulate her new colleague on her promotion (friendly eyes).
> Realize that she had not presented herself strongly enough in her interview (good mistakes). She arranges a meeting with the person who didn't appoint her to the job, and enquires in a friendly way about his or her reasons, and what she might be able to do in order to stand a better chance next time (curiosity and self-knowledge).
> She decides to train the necessary skills (self-discipline) and accept the situation as it is.
> In short, she shows courage and that is why she can accept the situation 'as it is' and 'not as she wants it to be'.

Acceptance is an active attitude, in contrast to indifference, which is passive. Acceptance increases your flexibility, whereas indifference limits it. Acceptance leads to peace and self-confidence. Indifference destroys your self-confidence and turns people off. When you experience a disappointment, it may be a good idea to remain silent. Why complain every time? You can choose not to react to a disappointment – instead, you simply observe the situation and realize that the feeling will pass. If you do that, the significance you attach to the situation will spring from wisdom, not from emotion.

Calm observation produces a sense of distance, from which position you can make a decision. Acceptance liberates the ego.

If we reflect on the meaning of the word courage again, we might be brave enough to look in the mirror to realize that we are often not capable of observing non-judgmentally.

Transparency and courage

Acceptance is sometimes hard to come by when there's a lack of transparency combined with courage. Sometimes, acceptance – if combined with silence or a failure to react – may confuse matters and be counter-productive, because there is no clarity about your position. Transparency involves the realization that it's impossible to arrive at acceptance without clarity, integrity and confidence. Show courage, and say what's on your mind, from a position of friendly eyes. Be specific about the problems. Acceptance should never be used as an excuse to leave problems unaddressed. In other words, acceptance without transparency is not true acceptance. You can say what's bothering you in a friendly, non-aggressive way. If you want to bring something up that you're unhappy about, you can start off with a non-judgmental phrase like 'can you help me to understand how that happened?'

An example

At a meeting, someone keeps monopolizing the discussion
and getting all the attention. No one else has a chance to say
anything. You think this is unfair, because it's an important
issue and it's supposed to be a team consultation. You can
choose: either you accept it and stop feeling annoyed, or
you show courage by intervening and giving your own
point of view. You say in a friendly way, but quite clearly:
'Can I have everyone's attention, please?' You wait until
everyone is looking at you, and then you carry on, talking
in a friendly voice: 'I think it's important that we hear
everyone's opinion at this meeting.'

When it comes to eye contact and the attention people bestow on
others, much of this is completely unconscious. You may feel that
people are ignoring you, or paying too little attention to you, to
your partner or to someone else. But this is often quite uninten-
tional. Pointing it out in a friendly fashion can sometimes make a
sea-change in their behaviour.

Another example

A customer is waiting to be served in a shop, while the two shop assistants are sitting loudly chatting and laughing together. The customer can choose to accept this, refusing to get irritated and go his own way, or he can choose to ask one of the shop assistants, in a friendly way, if one of them will serve him. Then he has done all he could do, even if he still isn't served properly after making his remark. He has displayed courage by making his position clear, as a customer. If the shop assistants choose to carry on giggling, he accepts it. If he hadn't said anything, he wouldn't have found out whether it was possible for him to be served here in a customer-friendly, attentive way. Of course, the shop assistants might well apologize and attend to him in a correct fashion.

By showing courage and taking action, you create clarity and from doing this comes acceptance.

As soon as you notice or feel that some minor, unimportant detail is niggling away at you, you know it's time for courage and transparency.

When there's an 'important' and sensitive issue at stake, it is obviously essential to take some time for reflection, but that doesn't change the fact that you'll also need courage and transparency in order to arrive at acceptance.

Compassion

Like gratitude (friendly eyes) and forgiveness (good mistakes), compassion is a skill that you can develop. Compassion is linked to acceptance. You accept your fellow human beings by not judging their behaviour but by showing empathy: putting yourself in the other person's position. When you see someone else's pain, you can sympathize, feel a sense of empathy. This will neutralize anger, hatred, aversion and even disgust.

A story is told about a pupil and cousin of Buddha who once asked the master if it was true to say that developing loving kindness and compassion was part of their doctrine. Buddha answered that it would be untrue to say that developing these qualities was part of their doctrine. It would be true to say that it was the whole of their doctrine.

Compassion leads to a stronger sense of connectedness with your environment. Furthermore, it helps you appreciate that your own situation is relatively positive, which leads to a sense of gratitude. And this in turn – as we discussed under the heading of 'gratitude' – makes you happier. If you convert compassion into actions, you'll also receive gratitude from others. All this produces stronger ties with those around you and fosters friendship. A great many positive effects can be produced by compassion: you learn to listen better and less judgmentally, you learn to deal better with disappointment, you arrive at a more positive self-image, and you find it easier to accept yourself.

1970s hippies?

Compassion is a precondition for 'connecting'. Oh yes, we know that lots of people feel a strong aversion to this term. It's had a bad press; it conjures up a bearded hippie from the 1970s. Even so, we want to mention it here. Because connecting with the people around us is a principle that impinges on every fibre of the Mindset method. Without it, applying the pillars would be a sterile and introverted business, shutting ourselves off from the outside world.

ACTIONS for ACCEPTANCE

1   Here's an exercise that is thousands of years old. Decide
    to exercise compassion today. Every time you meet
    someone from your immediate environment, or even
    when you encounter someone in the street, cultivate the
    thought: 'I want this person to be happy.' You'll notice
    an immediate change in your mood and your feeling.

2   Decide today to exercise transparency and courage. Is
    there a situation in your life, right now, that is unclear
    and that keeps bothering you? Get straight to the
    point (courage) and ask, with compassion, for clarity
    (transparency). Make sure you get your timing right and
    that you don't embarrass the other person. Sometimes,
    of course, it may actually be better not to bring up a
    particular sensitive subject because the other person is
    not ready for it. That's a question of having insight into,
    and compassion with, the other person. If it turns out
    to be impossible to discuss the subject, accept it. That's
    also a form of courage.

THE CONCENTRATIONS

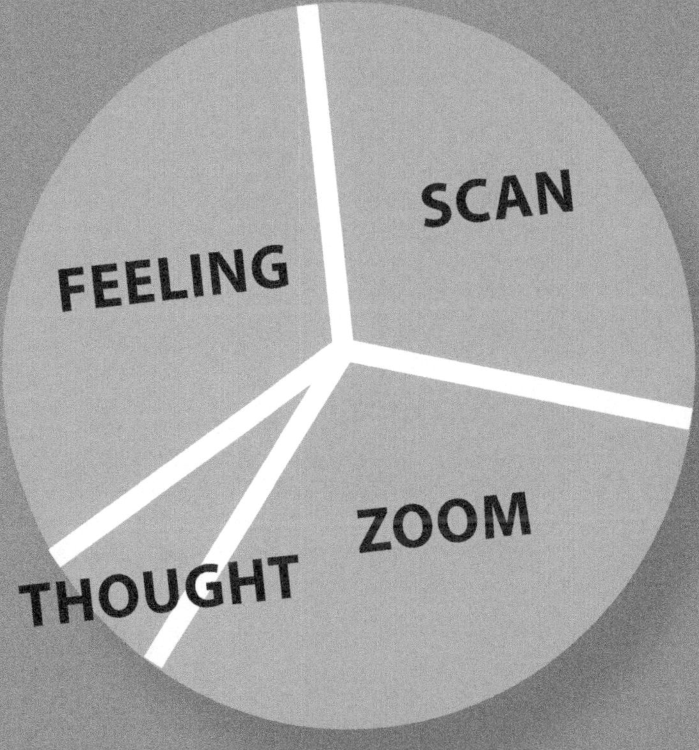

The four types of concentration come from professional sport, where the keyword is 'attention control'. Just as the pillars can help to train self-knowledge and self-management, the different types of concentration help to select and maintain your focus of attention. This too can be trained, as professional athletes are well aware. Perfect concentration means freedom from distraction. You can learn how to produce perfect concentration time and time again.

THE FOUR TYPES OF CONCENTRATION

SEARCHING FOR A BROOCH

The great theatre director and drama theorist Stanislavski descri-bes the following scene. A director asks an actress to act out the situation in which she is searching for a very valuable brooch that she has lost. She runs around the stage shaking her head, beating her breast in anguish. In the meantime she forgets to actually search for the brooch. She gets carried away, gets into a conside-rable panic, and is unconscious of exactly where her focus of at-tention is. The director asks her to look for the brooch again, and this time to really look for it. This time she looks purposefully, she is totally absorbed in her task, and the authenticity and focus of her quest are beyond question. The director explains that this is the right way to approach acting: it's not about pretending to do something, but about acting out real actions. The point is to know exactly what you want to concentrate on – and how.

The pioneering researcher here is the sports psychologist Robert Nideffer, who wrote the game-changing book Attention Control Training (1976). Our approach, which distinguishes between four types of concentration, is indebted to Nideffer.

The four types of concentration
thoughts
feeling
scanning (visual)
zoom ing (visual)

Scanning and zooming are external concentrations; your attention is focused on the outside world. This is visual attention. Scanning is a wide gaze that takes in the entire surroundings. Zooming is focusing on specific details. Thoughts and feeling are internal concentration, your attention is focused on your 'inner world': thoughts, feelings and sensory experiences. Thoughts include not only short, clear thoughts, but also tactics, strategy, and analysis. These are thoughts that possess quality, not the noise of story thinking that frequently consists of rambling, diffuse thoughts. For now, it's enough to say that feeling primarily means body awareness. The tension in your muscles, your breathing, and your sensory perceptions. This is the subject of the next chapter.

In everyday life, you are constantly switching from one concentration form to another. The more consciously you learn to switch, the better you will learn to focus your attention where you want it. Let's take two examples to clarify the different types of concentration. Both involve drivers: one operating in action thinking, the other in story thinking. What is the difference between the two, in the way they focus their concentration?

Driving as an action thinker

ZOOMING

You see potholes in the road and notice many billboards advertising all kinds of different products. You observe without judging.

SCANNING

You take a brief glance in your rear view mirror and see that the car behind you is beginning to overtake even though it is not allowed on this stretch of the road. You also see an oncoming car coming towards you at high speed. You observe without judging.

THOUGHTS

You estimate the distance between the car overtaking you and the oncoming car and you lower your speed accordingly, whilst also avoiding the potholes. This is strategy: thoughts.

FEELING

You put your foot gently but firmly on the brake, so that you can make room for the car that is overtaking you. Then you give a little gas. You speed up again, whilst enjoying the feeling of the wind passing through your hair, as the window is open. This is body awareness, 'feeling'.

Driving as a story thinker

ZOOMING

You see potholes in the road and notice numerous billboards advertising all kinds of different products. Both the potholes and the billboards really irritate you.

You link judgmental thoughts to your zooming.

SCANNING

You take a brief glance in your rear view mirror and see, to your disbelief, that the car behind you is mad enough to try and overtake you now, even though it is not allowed on this stretch of the road. Not only that, you also see an oncoming car approaching at a ridiculous speed. You consider both drivers total idiots. You observe and judge.

THOUGHTS

You decide to slow down to avoid an accident. You'd rather speed up, just to show both drivers what maniacs they really are, but that is too dangerous. Better to catch the driver up who overtook you later and overtake him yourself so that you can give him a filthy look and cut him off. You are now completely taken up with judgmental thoughts.

FEELING

You slam on the brakes, grasp the steering wheel as hard as you can. Your breathing is fast and shallow, your shoulders hunched forward. You realize your face is distorted into a grimace. This is lack of bodily awareness, 'feeling'.

What strikes you about what happens when 'judgmental observation' (story thinking) starts playing a role when you're driving? What happens to your concentration? What happens to your 'feeling', your body? What is your concentration focused on now? Do you realize that your mood affects your concentration and you concentration affects your mood?

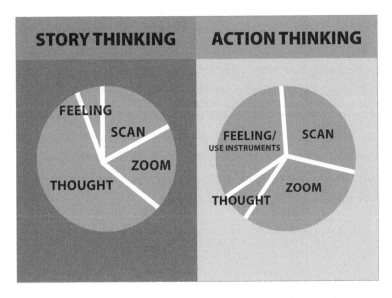

The image shows that in the case of the story-thinking driver, thoughts use up most of his mental energy. Thoughts prevail over the other types of concentration. Judgmental thoughts take the place of scanning, zooming and feeling. As a result, the concentration is directed entirely inward, and this impairs his ability to observe sharply. This influences the quality of his decisions.

On the right-hand side of the image, concentration has the freedom to be directed outwards – in *scanning* and *zooming* – because *thoughts* arising from action thinking are purposeful and non-judgmental. This enables the driver to gain faster and easier access to 'feeling' instead of getting bogged down in 'thoughts', as in the case of story thinking.

We can conclude that your concentration will often suffer from a surplus of thoughts. You can change this, first and foremost by realizing how often your concentration is disrupted by story thinking and secondly by not allowing this to irritate you. That's why we always take friendly eyes and good mistakes as the basis. By constantly starting off in the now, by realizing what your attention is focused on and how you are looking, you'll acquire more self-knowledge and gradually achieve more. And this will also impact on the people around you.

What does concentration look like in action thinking?

THOUGHTS

I decide to perform a certain action or to set a particular goal. These are clear, brief thoughts, which are invested with quality. 'I'll call Jef to discuss the conflict between us.'

FEELING

I switch to my body, feel the muscles of my face, my shoulders, I'm conscious of my breathing, body language, posture, and the way I'm using my voice. 'Before I pick up the phone, I'll slow down my breathing and sit down, feeling relaxed but attentive. My eyes and the muscles of my face are relaxed. I'm aware of how I'm going to use my voice.'

SCANNING AND ZOOMING

I know the precise focus of my gaze, whether it's a person, a thing or an event. I know the way in which, and for how long, I've been looking. I choose to scan (looking in the wide area around me) or to zoom (specifically targeted visual attention), depending on what is called for in the situation at hand. 'I won't allow my gaze to wander off, since I want to focus all my attention on the conversation.'

With this approach, I'm conscious of how I manage myself and perform actions based on feeling (because I'm conscious of my body) instead of on thoughts.

The key to the Mindset method is switching to observation (scanning and zooming) on the basis of feeling instead of thoughts.

As we noted above, the next chapter will be entirely taken up with 'feeling', which we regard as the most crucial type of concentration. Not because scanning, zooming and thoughts are less important, but because it's through feeling that we can shift to action thinking.

Now that we've finished dealing with the pillars and the four types of concentration, we hope that the reader understands that they are inextricably connected. As we said before, they are the two wings of the bird. If one doesn't work, the bird can't fly.

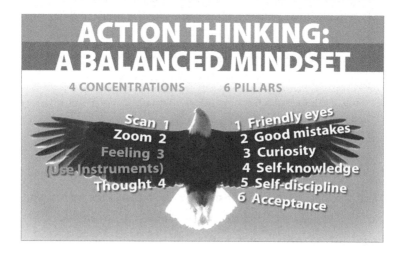

**ACTION THINKING:
A BALANCED MINDSET**

4 CONCENTRATIONS   6 PILLARS

Scan 1   1 Friendly eyes
Zoom 2   2 Good mistakes
Feeling 3   3 Curiosity
(Use Instruments)   4 Self-knowledge
Thought 4   5 Self-discipline
                         6 Acceptance

FEELING INSTEAD OF THOUGHT

THE BODY AS A VEHICLE

If the heart could think, it would stand still
– FERNANDO PESSOA: The Book of Disquiet

Finding it hard to get up in the morning, not being able to decide what to do today, not being able to motivate yourself to go to the gym today, dreading this afternoon's meeting. These are familiar feelings for everyone. You're stuck in story thinking and it seems that something is preventing you from taking action.

Body awareness

The magical key word to shift into action thinking is *feeling*. In our method, 'feeling' equals 'physical consciousness' and the awareness that you can use your body like a vehicle. Perhaps you have heard the expression 'motion is emotion'. We would agree. What it means is that by being conscious of your body, you can influence your emotions, thoughts, and hence also your reactions. In this way – and this is tangible – you can indirectly train the quality of your thoughts and learn to make choices in your emotions.

This is how top athletes work to constantly keep themselves focused in the here and now. And how they learn to deal with stress.

Everyone knows intuitively what it means to 'feel good'. The examples listed below will make you realize that you can use your body to influence your thoughts. You can become conscious of the emotions you have. This consciousness helps enable you to choose which thoughts you want to identify with.

You can easily train body awareness. Yoga, breathing techniques and meditation are all exercises in body awareness. Our experience with sport has taught us that if you don't shift from thought to 'feeling', your concentration will be poor and you won't perform well. There is a good reason that the great tennis player Novak Djokovic has made yoga into part of his daily routine, in order to find 'mental peace', as he says himself. He says that he had noticed his breathing becoming irregular under pressure and that yoga has helped to solve this problem. If one of the best tennis players in the world has difficulty breathing when under pressure, it seems quite likely that the rest of us have trouble with our breathing when we're under pressure. But our consciousness is often pitched so low that we don't even notice.

How you breathe is of vital importance in all sorts of situations involving feeling. From quarrels to deadlines, from fetching the children from school to job interviews, from giving presentations to watching a thriller. In fact it really applies to everything we do. Our breathing gets faster and becomes high and superficial if we feel that we're under pressure of some kind; this disrupts the quality of our thoughts and sometimes triggers undesirable reaction and emotions.

An example that could serve as a metaphor for 'feeling' is the titanic struggle between Nicolas Mahut and John Isner, in the third round of Wimbledon 2010, the longest tennis match ever played (11 hours and 5 minutes). The fifth set ended in 70-68. How can anyone carry on performing at the highest possible level for such a long period of time? Of course, countless thoughts will have come into these men's minds, but as superb athletes, they knew not to identify with them. By constantly using their body as a vehicle, they chose to shift their focus to their body for the entire duration of the match. We're referring here to breathing, eye control, lightness of movement and muscular tension. This enabled them to play with pure concentration instead of allowing the many thoughts of story thinking to influence them, and they succeeded in staying in the here and now and playing one point at a time.

Of course, the long-term goal might have been winning Wimbledon, but if they had focused on that goal, they would have lost their control over the moment, as well as their 'body awareness'. You can't directly influence the future, but you can influence how you use your body. If they had mainly focused on 'winning' (future), they would have got lost in thoughts; their physical pain and mental exhaustion would immediately have taken over. By staying in the here and now, they remained alert and in action thinking throughout the match. It was an amazing achievement.

Another great example from sport. Rafael Nadal, the world famous tennis player, takes a cold shower before every big match. He wants to start the match with a feeling of total alertness. By going through this fairly extreme ritual, he literally shifts himself from thought to feeling.

These last two examples may seem rather remote from our lives. Even so, there's no doubt at all that we're frequently completely oblivious to our physical state. Lack of body awareness is very common. It not only causes shoulder, neck and back problems. It also leads to mental discomfort.

Let us give you one last example that might be easier to recognize. This is an example of how 'feeling' instead of 'thought' can work on the company floor.

At the beginning of meetings, we coach the managers to ask everyone around the boardroom table to close their eyes and lower their breathing for one minute. The outcome of this, is that everyone involved is calmer, more alert and present then they were one minute earlier. The meeting begins in action thinking.

It is important to realise the impact of these minimalistic actions.

ACTION for FEELING

Something we all know and yet constantly forget: you're sitting at your desk and you realize that your posture is tense. You notice that your shoulders are hunched or tight. Decide straight away, with friendly eyes, to focus on your shoulder and neck muscles. Relax. Make sure your breathing is calm and deep. Feel the tension ebb away from your shoulders. What's the position of your feet? Are both feet flat on the floor? Is your back straight? If necessary, stand up for a minute, walk away from your desk energetically, walk with an erect posture, briefly raise your shoulders and then let them go. Feel the increase of energy with every step you take, put your feet down consciously, feel the floor beneath your feet. In this way you can reset your mindset to feeling. All this may sound a bit obvious, but if you apply it consistently, you'll find that it feels different and that it immediately influences your mindset.

El sueño de la razón produce monstruos.

BATS, OWLS AND MONSTERS

SO, DOES ALL THIS MEAN THAT
THOUGHTS ARE UNIMPORTANT?

A famous etching by the Spanish painter Francisco de Goya is called *El sueño de la razón produce monstruos*: 'The sleep of reason produces monsters'. It's a self-portrait of the artist, in which he has fallen asleep with his head on his desk. Swarming around him are bats and owls, monsters looming out of the dark at him with wide-open, luminous eyes. The image shows what happens in the absence of reason. Without reason, we may change into aimless monsters; where reason sleeps, we can expect doom and disaster.

We have said again and again that thoughts may have the effect of paralyzing, frustrating or disrupting our actions. Does that mean they're unimportant? Absolutely not. Reason, analysis, planning, reflection and self-reflection are important and necessary, especially when linked to action. But getting bogged down in thoughts that are not linked to any real action will often lead to story thinking, with all the negative consequences that ensue. Of course, it may sometimes be useful to 'shelve' ideas and thoughts, so that we can devote attention to them later, when the time is right.

Take the following example. A mother and father are having problems dealing with their teenage son. It's extremely important to think about these problems. Reflection and analysis are useful to make a start on solving the problems. But reflection and analysis alone will not change anything. 'Thoughts' need to pass over the bridge of 'feeling' to lead to action. That bridge may be, for instance, visualizing a conversation with the teenager. How do the parents envisage that conversation? What tone of voice will they use? How do they expect and want to feel? How do they expect their child to feel? What would be the best way of tackling it, when and where should they do so? How do they see themselves reacting? How do they see their child reacting? What result do they expect to achieve?

Thoughts that are valuable often lead to some kind of action. If other, irrelevant, thoughts arise, you don't need to identify with them. Let them go, just as the surfing guru doesn't try to stop the waves, but does learn to move with them. Or, in the words of this book's motto: 'Action is about living fully. Inaction is the way that we deny life.'

YOU HAVE (NOT) REACHED
YOUR DESTINATION

A SMALL DIGRESSION

That this is a good place to insert a little digression about the difference between goals and destination [NB The word destination is used here in different senses here, one being the older sense of purpose or destiny – transl.]. You might say that the pillars help to set the course towards your destination and the different types of concentration help you achieve your goals.

We believe that a goal can be achieved: a house, a job, promotion, and so on. But you can't reach your destination. You can be on your way to achieving a goal, but you can't be on your way to your destination. Your destination is what you consider valuable in life. In our eyes, your values can only be lived through, not achieved. Your values focus on the now, whereas your goals will generally focus on the future. Values are your foundation. They give you something to hold onto, and help you to weather the storms.

At the end of his life, the American poet and novelist Conrad Aiken went back to Savannah, Georgia, where he had been born. He loved going on walks with his wife along the riverside to look at the ships. On one of these walks, they saw a ship called 'Cosmos

Mariner' sailing down the Savannah River towards the sea. When they got home, they searched in the newspapers for the ship's destination, but the destination was listed as 'Unknown'. Aiken asked his wife to put this on his grave. He died in 1973. His gravestone, in the famous Bonaventure Cemetery, is fashioned in the shape of a marble bench, with the inscription:

COSMOS MARINER
DESTINATION UNKNOWN

The anecdote suggests that you might never be able to reach your destination. Even when the soul has left the body.

Life is full of goals, from redecorating the kitchen or purchasing a new car to getting a new degree. Becoming famous, making a lot of money, or winning cups also come under the heading of goals. Destination, in the sense of purpose, is something different. This has to do with the 'why' of our lives, the core values from which we want to operate. This 'why' may well be the engine of all our actions. It's the ethical principle on which we base our actions, the soul or beating heart of our actions. We don't work – as in the case of a goal – towards a destination. On the contrary, the destination helps to guide all our actions in the here and now. This destination is also personal, and is determined by the values that each person considers important. Values might include: beauty, love, openness, wisdom, adventure, independence, friendship, challenges, creativity, tolerance, and so on. You can't reach your destination or purpose in the same way that you can achieve a goal. It will influence the actions you take and how you take them at every moment in time.

We may want to decide where we want to go, but we can never know precisely where that is, and where it will lead us. It's good to realize, in this context, that it's more important how we feel when we achieve something than precisely what we get. Action thinking also means that we constantly undertake action and don't dwell endlessly on what's going on in our head in relation to what we're trying to achieve. Our destination is always in the now, and in the feeling we experience with our actions.

Questions concerning your destination/purpose

1. What personal values do you consider important when you phone your parents?
   For example: loyalty, independence, openness, respect, thoughtfulness.
2. What personal values do you consider important when you're at work with your colleagues?
   For example: pleasure, justice, creativity, appreciation, integrity.

Questions concerning your goals

1. What do you want to achieve when you call your parents?

   For example: Agree a date for a birthday meal. Can you help out with the redecoration of the bathroom? Is there something you can take with you from town on your next visit?

2. What do you want to achieve at work?

   For example: Finish your project before the deadline. Consult a colleague about a new work location.

   Get some advice about how to present something at the next conference.

On the next page you see a summary of the Mindset method. Story thinking and action thinking, the pillars, the concentrations and also the instruments. We will be handling the instruments that chase away the mosquitoes in the next chapters. As explained at the beginning of the book, the Mindset method works in four steps:

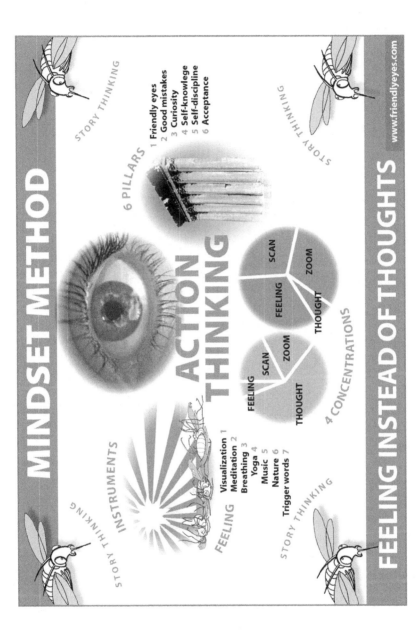

THE INSTRUMENTS

You have reached your destination . . .
or not?

Is our story starting to sound like a
flower-power message from the 1970s?
Let's ditch the incense and get
back to some practical advice.
The next few chapters look at
7 instruments to keep the annoying,
pointless mosquitoes at bay. They are aids
to conjuring up the right feeling. They
are simple, tangible and practical. We all
know them, but often forget to use them.

THE INSTRUMENTS

INTRODUCTION

Sensational or down-to-earth?

The instruments can be used on a daily basis to help you live a life guided by feeling instead of thoughts. They can help induce mental tranquillity.

Many of us frequently find ourselves overstretched, with busy schedules and too little energy. It would be good if there were a way of feeling less pressure and tapping new sources of energy. Fortunately, there is a way of doing so – by using the instruments recommended here as part of your daily life.

Story thinking keeps you unconsciously shackled to what seems an automatic routine, the path of ignorance. As a result, you act out the same patterns every day. Patterns that consume energy and that may induce nervous tension, frustration, and dissatisfaction. The action thinker, on the other hand, is constantly willing to break with old habits, to use instruments to tap new energy sources, and to act on the basis of feeling. Essentially, living like this can build up new habits of mind that generate energy.

We would like to mention here that our first book *Mindset, a mental guide for sport,* also uses instruments. But these instruments are applied to sport and that is the reason for not mentioning them here. Although there are great similarities.

> **The seven instruments for mental tranquillity**
> visualization, meditation, breathing exercises, yoga, music, nature, trigger words & mantras

Let's start with the first four instruments, since these are often seen as complicated.
Visualization, meditation, breathing exercises and yoga are not spectacular new inventions, although they are often discussed in a rather sensationalist way or linked to mysticism. We would prefer to describe them in a practical, down-to-earth way. They are skills that you can only muster if you practice them regularly for an extended period of time. If you use them every day, you will experience directly the ways in which they release energy and how this will influence your mood and focus.

It's important to get a clear idea of what precisely each individual instrument involves:
1. Meditation is observing things as they are.
2. Breathing exercises are used as a conscious means of relaxation or acquiring more energy.

3. Visualization is seeing what you want to achieve and how you want to be.
4. Yoga is both meditation (observing things as they are), breathing (using your breathing consciously to relax your body) and practising the concentration type feeling (body awareness).

What 'benefits' can you derive from these four instruments, and what are the essential differences between them?

The difference between meditation and visualization

Meditation helps you anchor yourself in the here and now. You focus your attention solely on what is there. Meditation feels like you are doing nothing, but it's actually the opposite. Meditation is an active, intensive kind of work. It prepares you for a mindset that allows space for acceptance and compassion. It's observing things as they are.

Visualization is seeing situations that are specifically different from the situation you are in now. It's about imagining situations that have not yet come about. Paradoxically, however, visualization itself takes place totally in the here and now, while you're mentally preparing yourself for the future. You conjure up situations in which you behave differently, react differently, experience different feelings or in which the circumstances are different compared to the present. While you're visualizing, you experience these images as if the situations were actually taking place now. You're the director. You expect what you visualize to turn into reality. You experience the imagined situations as real and tangible.

The difference between breathing and meditation

In meditation you merely observe 'things as they are'. This means that you observe your breathe in it's natural state. If your breathing is rapid, it's rapid. If it's slow, it's slow. If it's shallow, it's shallow.

With breathing exercises you consciously influence your breathing. You choose to lower your breathing, to achieve relaxation. Alternatively, you may consciously choose to speed up your breathing in order to produce more energy.

In a nutshell: breathing exercises consciously influence the rhythm of your natural breathing, whereas with meditation you merely observe your natural breathing.

In our view, yoga is a combination of 'feeling' (body awareness), breathing exercises and meditation.

We see yoga as dynamic meditation. By becoming conscious of what your body is doing, you shift your attention to the here and now. This helps you look at yourself, while using the pillar 'acceptance'. The teacher, and other students, might be much more flexible, experienced, focused and so on than you are. But that's not where your attention should be. Only a very small part of yoga is about becoming physically more flexible. In yoga, by far the most important point is to be constantly trying, learning to use your breathing perfectly, learning to find the right position. It goes without saying that you won't find the right position, or be able to control your breathing straight away. But by staying in the here and now, accepting yourself as you are, seeing your physical limitations as they are and not experiencing them as limitations, you will also be practising meditation.

In a nutshell: yoga is a combination of meditation, breathing exercises, and body awareness.

Research has shown that the benefits to be gained from meditation, breathing exercises and yoga include the following:

1. Lower blood pressure
2. Slower heart rate and breathing
3. Better circulation
4. Stronger immune system
5. A reduction in chronic pain
7. A balanced mood

VISUALIZATION

DAYDREAM OR DESTINATION?

The book *Mindset* dealt at length with a number of instruments used by world-class sportsmen and sportswomen to get to the right feeling of action thinking. In this chapter we shall be looking at this subject in more depth, discussing ways of how visualization, in particular, can be used to train action thinking in daily life.

Visualization means thinking in images, conjuring up a situation in your mind's eye. Many people say they find this difficult. And yet we use visualization every day. We daily conjure up situations in our minds that have not yet happened. Everyone develops his or her own patterns in the way they worry, for instance, about things like money, their jobs or house, their relationship or children, tax demands and so on. That is also thinking in images. Everyone feels anxiety or worries, and some people also see their anxiety in images. What stops us conjuring up different images and feelings? You can replace the images you normally see every day with new images, chosen intentionally, situations that correspond with your values and influence your mood positively. There is a well-known saying, 'If you can see it, you can be it'. Visualization can produce this change.

Suppose you conjure up an image of a situation in the future. This also means conjuring up the emotions you would have in that situation. You literally see what is happening in front of your eyes. You visualize instead of verbalizing. This gives a sense of calm and prevents you giving way to panic or anxiety in the real situation.

Two examples of visualization
1. You have to write a complicated report.
Story thinking: You think that you are not capable of writing the report well. The more you think about it, the more things occur to you that might go wrong or that you're not good at. Eventually you don't see any way at all of getting the report finished or written well. It looms over you, weighing you down.
Action thinking: You see before you that you enjoy figuring out the sentences. You realize that you're capable of doing this. And even though it's a challenge, you feel the fun and the excitement of tackling such a complicated assignment. You visualize yourself putting the last full stop at the end of the report and reading it through with great satisfaction.

2. You have to tell an assistant an unpleasant piece of news. Your assistant has been working overtime without telling you about it. It turns out there is no budget to pay for the overtime.

Story thinking: You dread having to tell your assistant this news and try not to think about it because it seems somewhat unfair to you. You can't get it out of your mind. You don't dare tell the assistant that the overtime can't be paid, and you're sure that she assumes it will be. You keep imagining your assistant getting angry or being incredibly disappointed in you. You're afraid to lose her, since she's an excellent employee.

Action thinking: You see yourself starting up the conversation. You feel and know that your intentions are good and that you have your assistant's best interests at heart. Then you see the following scene clearly in your mind's eye: you are breathing calmly and looking at your assistant with friendly eyes. You practise what you're going to say and how that feels. For instance, 'I'd like to speak to you about the overtime you've been doing. Have you got a moment, some time today?' Later on, when you've planned the meeting with her, you see yourself saying: 'I understand that you thought that you would be paid for your overtime, is that right?'

Assuming that she answers yes, you see and hear yourself say: 'I'm very sorry, but we don't have the budget to pay for that overtime. Of course I'm happy with all your work and everything you've achieved, but I wasn't aware that you were doing overtime, and I'm afraid I just don't have the resources for it this time. Let's agree that next time you consult me first before you begin with overtime work. In that way I don't have to disappoint you again like this.' This gives her space to express disappointment and anger, if that's what she feels, and you accept what she decides after hearing this 'unfair' piece of news. Alternatively, you might be pleasantly surprised, if she is able to display understanding for your position. Whichever way it goes, you accept her reaction and take it in your stride. You've shown courage and the situation is transparent. You can imagine the person being shocked at first, but eventually being grateful for your tact and honesty.

The feeling that you 'Must Have This Horrible Talk' always works counterproductively. Make sure you prevent this feeling from arising, by seeing the situation as completely normal. Feel the emotions that go with the exchange. The more details you see in your mind's eye, the better it will work. The calmer you envisage yourself reacting, the calmer you will be.

There's no such thing as falling . . . in visualization

Epke Zonderland attained a historic achievement at the London Olympics by winning gold with a sequence that had never been done before. He says he constantly uses visualization: he can see all the actions in his mind before he does them. He says: 'Once I started visualizing my different flight elements, I became calmer.' Four years earlier, Epke fell when he tried the same sequence at the Beijing Olympics. So you might think that his visualization didn't work. But Epke carried on visualizing himself carrying out the exercise flawlessly, day after day. He disregarded the 'reality' that the sequence frequently went wrong, focusing instead on what he wanted to achieve. He conjured up the image of performing the three flight elements perfectly, back-to-back.

No-stress visualization

Suppose that Epke Zonderland's visualizations had only focused on money and fame, instead of the perfect execution of the movements. Then these visualizations would have come with a great deal of stress. In our view, money and fame are not linked to a destination or purpose in life, but to a materialistic goal. These goals are also fine if you use the right values to achieve them. Epke has said that he wanted to perform to the best of his ability, with the help of his team and his family. All this has to do with a purpose in life. Achieving your purpose in life may bring you money and fame, which may be one of your goals. But it was Epke's values and his close bond with his family and his team that kept Epke's passion in equilibrium. Of course he also wanted the gold medal, and was prepared to take any risk to achieve it. But that was not the only or primary motive that drove him.

Without taking action, visualization is self-deception

People often have dream images of the future without linking them to actions through visualization. They might dream of an amazing promotion at work, of opening a Bed & Breakfast in France, or of buying a house in Greece. Day in, day out, their life is composed of the same patterns, alternating with fragments of these dreams. In fact these fragments of virtual future happiness are a kind of numbing drug. They generate a constant feeling of frustration. Here, the visualization is a lie. That is because there's a lack of willingness to make the necessary effort and preparations to actually achieve these dreams (and to visualize these intermediate steps too). You want to take that important step on the moon without all the smaller preparatory steps that have to be taken first. What do you have to do to earn that promotion, to open that B&B, or to acquire that house? These steps are simply left out. In the chapter 'You have (not) reached your destination' we wrote that your destination, in the sense of your life purpose, should be in the here and now. When you visualize your future, you can link it to your intentions and your personal values.

It's only by adopting this attitude that you will acquire energy, satisfaction and passion, not by cherishing a vague, materialistic vision of the future. You take action: you learn French, you follow courses at work that will give you a real chance of getting that promotion. That in itself will provide satisfaction, even if you never get that B&B in France or that amazing promotion you had hoped for or the house in Greece. Satisfaction only exists in the here and now. Be pleased with what you achieve with your actions. The important point is how you feel when you achieve something, not what you get for it. Link everything you want to your values. Stephen Covey wrote in his book *The Seven Habits of Highly Effective People* that everyone who is searching for that destination, that purpose, must ask himself the following question: 'What do you want people to say at your funeral?' It would surely be a bit peculiar if you wanted your best friend to say at your funeral: 'He was a terrific guy. He bought a house in Greece and owned two beautiful cars.'

Visualization and comfort zone

Visualization is empty and pointless if you aren't prepared to leave your comfort zone. What we mean by this is that you will have to perform certain actions that you wouldn't normally perform. For your B&B, for instance, you'll need to set up a website. You have no idea how to set up a website. You'd rather not think about it; it's not your thing. That's a perfect way of fooling yourself: reacting to everything outside your comfort zone with 'it's not my sort of thing' or 'I don't know anything about that'. You'd rather carry on doing what you're used to. And yet you still expect to somehow turn your dream into reality. Clearly, this is totally unrealistic, and it highlights the difference between daydreaming and visualization.

How would you use visualization, for instance, in this B&B example, and stop it remaining a daydream?
See the website in your mind's eye: it's up and running. See your future customers surfing the web, googling 'unique Bed & Breakfast in Limousin'. They immediately find your B&B 'Piece of Paradise' in Limousin. You envisage the happy faces of those website visitors when they look at the lovely photos of the modern rooms. You see them carrying on clicking to see the pictures of the surrounding countryside. Then you go further still: you see yourself and your partner welcoming guests as they arrive. You offer them a cup of tea or coffee, or a glass of fresh orange juice. You take them to their room, where there's a fresh smell and the bed is nicely made up. There are soft towels and tablets of local soap on the bed. The people are enthusiastic and happy to have found your B&B.

You do all this to ensure that your visualization will be translated into reality. Otherwise it will remain an empty daydream. You also visualize the steps that must be taken to make that dream come true.

People frequently claim that they don't really know what they want. This makes it hard to visualize anything. That is sometimes because the ultimate goal is too ambitious or unrealistic. Alternatively, perhaps your ultimate goal is not linked to your destination, your purpose in life, as a result of which it feels wrong and doesn't give you sufficient pleasure. Both will take away your energy and you will feel a lack of motivation.

If you always link what you want to visualize to your values, then you'll always do the right thing and you'll be able to produce the passion and energy to take all the necessary action, again and again, to achieve it.

This approach will make it fun to set up your own website. Thoughts and images that hold you back will vanish. That's because each step now has significance and is connected to the chosen destination or purpose. The mosquitoes of story thinking will disappear, making way for the star of action thinking. Visualization is easy to train. You can use the 'art of action' explained later on.

ACTION

What does your life look like in 1 year's time? Five years' and ten years' time?

Describe how you see it, how it feels, where you are, who is with you, what you look like, what your partner does or who your partner is – assuming that you want a partner.

What practical actions might you perform today that relate directly to the visualization of your life in one year, five years' or ten years' time?

This action takes a lot of time. It is perfectly normal to take several months to develop your plan.

You can go to our free online video mental training course 'Discover' to get help and tips on how to visualize and more www.friendlyeyes.com

MEDITATION

TRAINING ATTENTION

Meditation is observing things as they are. It's training attention. That may sound boring, and make us feel like we don't want to do it. Or it may sound like a pointless waste of time. You'd rather undertake some action. Or you may wish meditation could provide something sensational, a spectacular experience. Some people may actually think they can't meditation. But if you say, 'I can't meditate', you're basically saying something much like 'I can't breathe'. Meditation is essentially working – working actively and intensively. When you are meditating and hard at work ensuring that you are both alert and relaxed at the same time, you may often get the feeling that you're not getting anything out of it. Quite the opposite is true, you're getting more than you can imagine out of it. The following story will clarify the point of meditation.

A ten-day experience

Like so many people, Jackie was intrigued by meditation and searching for inner peace. In 2002 she came across a ten-day meditation course of Vipassana: see www.dhamma.org. She decided to spend ten days shifting her attention radically to the 'inner world'. The course involved meditating in a closed environment for ten hours a day, without making eye contact, without speaking, without pen and paper, without the noise of cars, without a mobile phone. That seemed like a big challenge, and also a way of finding out whether meditation was really 'worth the trouble'. In the first three days of the course, the assignment is to focus solely on your natural breathing. This means sitting on your cushion for ten hours a day and only observing your breathing, without influencing it. Since Jackie found it very difficult to keep her attention focused on her breathing – even though it sounded like a simple assignment – she gradually felt she was balancing on the edge of madness. Looking back later, she felt that this was one of the best learning experiences she had ever had. This period of meditation, in which she had to move right outside her comfort zone, was for her the beginning of adopting a new philosophy of life.

After following several ten-day dhamma courses, one thing became crystal-clear to her: if you can focus your attention on one thing (your breathing) uninterruptedly for more than a few minutes, without any distracting thoughts intruding into your mind, you can almost call it a miracle. This exercise, in which you focus all your attention exclusively on the activity of inhaling and exhaling through your nose, is called Anapana meditation. Practising doing this, without the thoughts of story thinking constantly bringing you back to your 'everyday stuff', is far more of a challenge than you can imagine. Before you know it, for instance, your thoughts have returned to your childhood or to something that irritates you. Or you find yourself reproaching yourself for failing to keep your attention focused on your breathing. Or you feel physical discomfort (which you may at times be unconsciously imagining as a way of escaping from having to focus on your breathing!). But it takes several days, months or even years (or never) for you to realize this, and this happens when you first realize and experience what non-judgmental observation is. Essentially, the core of the Mindset method lies in the insights gained from sitting on a meditation mat during those Vipassana training sessions.

You can never take it for granted that you are truly 'attentive', even if you have set your sights on well-defined goals and you're doing your very best. Even dedicated, hard-working top athletes can't take it for granted that they are constantly keeping their attention in the right place. Jackie gradually realized this (with her own history as a professional tennis player) while she was trying to keep her attention focused on her breathing, and to her great irritation kept 'failing', again and again.

When she became aware of the frequently pointless thoughts that kept running through her head, it was an unpleasant confrontation. What is this voice, why doesn't it stop, and am I the only person troubled by so many rubbishy thoughts? Asking these questions in itself represents an initial moment of consciousness-raising, or even 'awakening'. You might describe it as 'a growing consciousness of a lack of consciousness.' This discovery leads to more acceptance in all sorts of everyday situations, which in turn leads to inner calm and self-confidence.

Meditation has proven its worth since time immemorial as a way of rediscovering peace within ourselves. So why not incorporate this technique into our everyday routine!

Exercise

Sitting meditation

It doesn't matter if you sit on a chair or a cushion. The most important thing is that you sit relaxed and focused at the same time. Choose a position that suits you and don't wish for something different.

Suppose you choose an upright chair. Place your feet flat on the ground, slightly apart. Rest your hands on your thighs or place them in your lap.

If you're sitting on a cushion or a little bench, cross your legs. Make sure that you feel comfortable. That means supporting your knees with a cushion if they stick up.

- Your back is as straight as a board, you're sitting alert and relaxed at the same time.
- Your neck and shoulders are relaxed.
- Your chin is pulled in a little.
- Your eyes are gently closed.
- Your facial muscles are relaxed.
- Your tongue is resting softly and low in your mouth.

Focus your attention on your natural breathing. You are breathing in and out through your nose. Do this for about two minutes. Feel your breath going in and out. Is the breath going through your left or your right nostril? Or through both? Observe your breathing just as it is. Don't form any judgments about it. Is your breath warmer or colder when you breathe in or out? Do you feel any difference in temperature?

Meditate like this every day for two minutes. That's a fine beginning. Carry on doing it for several months. If you want to meditate for longer that is fine, but avoid turning it into a competition. You'll notice that you begin to get used to the silence and the restful sensation. You'll also notice that you can evoke this state of mind, of observing without judging, more and more often in the course of the day. And it will get easier to conjure it up whenever you want to.

ADVICE for MEDITATION

If you really want to understand what meditation involves and what it could mean for you, practice daily for 12 weeks in our online meditation course. It's challenging, fun and it works. www.friendlyeyes.com

S.N. Goenka gives ten-day training courses in Vipassana, based on donations: www.dhamma.org

Jon Kabat-Zinn explains the principles of meditation at length in his book '*Wherever You Go, There You Are*'.

BREATHING

STRESSFUL OR CALM, CHEST OR ABDOMEN?

Breathing plays an important part in regulating tension and stress. Irregular breathing is an early sign of story thinking or of poor physical or mental health. The sooner you become aware of this irregularity, the sooner you can do something about it.

As soon as you focus on your breathing, you leave story thinking and automatically shift your attention to the here and now of action thinking. Past and future disappear. You feel directly connected to your body.

There are two sorts of breathing: shallow, chest breathing, and deeper, abdominal breathing. Abdominal breathing is more efficient and produces a calmer state of mind. It uses the diaphragm, enabling the inhaled air to penetrate deep into the lungs. This produces restful, deep breathing. Chest breathing only reaches the top part of the lungs, using only part of the lung capacity. Most people unconsciously use this shallow, chest breathing (they are unconsciously incompetent). By doing breathing exercises you can learn abdominal breathing (eventually becoming unconsciously competent), so that you are also able to breathe like this in stressful situations. Abdominal breathing helps you remain calm and avoid stress in all kinds of situations.

Better decisions

It will be obvious that you can make better decisions if you have your breathing under control and are able to breathe more deeply, whether consciously or unconsciously. Many top athletes practice awareness of their breathing for hours at a time, enabling them to make the right tactical decisions when they're under pressure. Experience this yourself by doing the following extremely simple exercise.

For the correct sitting posture, see the section on meditation.

Exercise

a. Count the number of natural breaths you take in 60 seconds. Inhale and exhale through your nose. Count one for each full cycle of inhalation and exhalation. Don't make your breathing shallower or deeper. It's not a competition. Just observe how many times you breathe in and out, without influencing it. There's no good or bad 'score' here.

b. Now decide to lower your breathing. Try to get down to somewhere between three and nine full breaths a minute. Do this by consciously inhaling and exhaling more deeply, still through your nose. Feel your diaphragm move up and down.

If you do this once or twice a day, you will find it easier to make decisions based on action thinking. If you and your fellow workers decide to start every meeting like this, everyone will start the meeting in a calmer and more alert frame of mind.

To really learn to regulate your breathing better, you need expert guidance. This is not the place to insert a long discussion on this subject; instead, we would like to bring your attention to one of the authorities on breathing techniques.

ADVICE for BREATHING

Professor Andrew Weil studied medicine and biology at Harvard University. He has made breathing exercises into his life's work. He discusses the how and why of these exercises at length in his practical audiobooks. His exercises help you experience what breathing can do with you, and his voice and clarity in guiding you through the exercises are inspiring.

You can order his Audio CD on Amazon (or in mp3 format through Audible): *Breathing: The Master Key to Self Healing*.

YOGA

STRETCHES YOUR MIND TOO!

Yoga is not an exotic sort of gymnastics that is only practised by mystical yogis in India. It's also not a special thing for middle-aged women coping with the menopause, men stuck in a midlife crisis, effeminate men or airy-fairy characters. Yoga is a practical, tangible way of training feeling and body awareness. It teaches you how to use your breathing and your body to switch from 'thoughts' to 'feeling'.

Many people find it difficult to tell the difference between tense and relaxed muscles. Yoga can teach you this. Yoga is a method that uses breathing and physical exercises to switch back and forth between effort and relaxation, both physical and mental. It teaches you how to focus your energy constructively and to calm down your story-thinking mind. Yoga also helps you to become conscious, at an earlier stage, of the emotions that may take hold of you. By doing breathing and physical exercises, you can learn to quickly recognize these emotions and decide what to do with them.

As you become more aware of your physical limitations and thresholds, you also learn to distinguish between different kinds of pain. You'll sometimes hear a distinction made between 'green' and 'red' pain. Green pain is pain that you should listen to – you shouldn't deny it – but that you don't have to react to. Red pain should immediately set alarm bells ringing; it generally warns you to stop doing whatever you're doing. You should never deny pain, since that will cause even more stress. With green pain, you can learn to relax. Yoga teaches you how to distinguish between different kinds of pain and helps you deal with them.

There are many different ways of practising yoga. In Western countries, Hatha yoga is the best known and commonest kind. It consists of physical exercises as well as exercises in breathing, balance, relaxation and concentration. The aim is to make you feel more balanced and energetic. An added advantage is that yoga improves your body's flexibility and helps to prevent injury.

Many athletes, performers and artistes have become aware of the benefits to be gained from yoga and have made it part of their daily lives. They know that their breathing is disrupted by pressure. If they find that their breathing is disrupted by pressure, it seems very likely that you and I experience the same thing. But it's quite possible that we're not aware of it. In the tennis world, Novak Djokovic and Maria Sharapova use yoga and the 'sun salutation' every day. In the entertainment world, Jennifer Aniston, Sting, Gwyneth Paltrow, Bon Jovi and many others say that daily yoga exercises give them a kind of balance that they would otherwise find impossible to attain in their busy lives.

Which form of yoga and why?

If you've never done yoga before, we would advise starting off with Iyengar yoga. This type of yoga focuses on a perfect technique, combined with attention to breathing. People who teach Iyengar yoga are usually highly trained and have many years of experience. It is quite common for yoga schools to allow students to practise poses in a totally irresponsible way, paying little or no attention to technical execution. This is dangerous and can cause permanent injuries.

Hatha yoga is also a good start. This is a slow form of yoga and is suitable for people with little or no experience.

We would advise against starting off with intensive and quicker forms of yoga, such as Ashtanga, Vinyasa, Bikram or Power Yoga. This is because we believe that the speed in which the poses are learnt and practised makes it very difficult for novices to learn the correct poses and become totally aware of their breathing. Of course for the more experienced practioner, these forms of yoga are excellent options.

Take care! Choose a teacher who has had years of experience practising yoga and who has followed a special training course for several years. If your teacher doesn't pay any attention to following your breathing during the lesson, or does not correct your posture, you know that this teacher is not competent.

If you really want to understand what yoga involves, go to the master B.K.S. Iyengar and read his book *Light on Yoga*. Schocken Books. New York, 1966

ACTION
Take a trial yoga lesson. See if you notice a difference in how you feel before and after the lesson. Choose your teacher carefully, shop around.

Here are three renowned yoga schools with highly-trained teachers in Amsterdam:
Iyengar Yoga bij Zeeburg; www. yogaber.nl
YogaGarden in de Jordaan; www.yogagarden.nl
Saimithra bij de Nieuwmarkt; www.saimithra.nl

Here are two renowned yoga schools with highly-trained teachers abroad:
CP Yoga in Lisbon (Portugal) and Valencia (Spain); www.cpyoga.com Teacher Carlos Rui
Iyengar Yoga in Cape Town (South Africa); www.yogateacher.co.za Teacher Meryl Urson

NATURE

THE GREEN MEDICINE

Just as music can change our mood, we can also benefit from spending time in natural surroundings. We often forget how simple it is to 'charge our batteries' by setting off into the fresh air for a walk or a bicycle ride, and enjoying the beautiful scenery.

The philosopher, poet and naturalist Henry David Thoreau writes in his diary:
'I love Nature partly because she is not man, but a retreat from him. None of his institutions control or pervade her. There a different kind of right prevails. In her midst I can be glad with an entire gladness. If this world were all man, I could not stretch myself, I should lose all hope. He is constraint, she is freedom to me. He makes me wish for another world. She makes me content with this.' (*Diary*, January 3, 1853)

Nature seems to offer the ideal surroundings in which to learn to be in the here and now, purely to observe without judging and to accept things as they are. 'As it is, not as you want it to be': in the great outdoors, that attitude almost goes without saying. That is the gist of the last two sentences in the quotation from Thoreau.

Like music, nature can reconcile us to existence. Nature is a perfect teacher of action thinking.

ACTION

Choose a date within the next four weeks to spend outdoors in the nature.

MUSIC

THE MELODIC MEDICINE

At the beginning of the 20th century, surgeons began to use music during operations, because they knew it would provide some distraction. Nowadays, we know that music can help to reduce pain, stress, and anxiety in a variety of ways. Research has even shown that less anaesthetic is needed if the patient is listening to music when being prepared for surgery. It works best with music that the patient likes and relates to. It also helps with recovery from a stroke, for instance, as well as speeding up the treatment of aphasia, alleviating pain, and reducing stress. Patients who listen to music during or after a surgical procedure need less sedation and experience less pain. Their heart rate and breathing become steadier and their blood pressure comes down.

It is common knowledge that music has a great effect on us. Even so, we often forget that it is a wonderful instrument for bringing us back to the feeling of action thinking and shifting us away from the diverse thoughts of story thinking. You can use music consciously as a means of conjuring up the 'right feeling'. Many top athletes listen to music before and during a match. It helps them concentrate and get into the 'right feeling'. Music can help you to silence the judgmental, critical voice in your head. It can also serve as a way of finding rhythm and balance. Music can calm and relax you, or it can revitalize and energize you. It's an important 'remedy' if you're having trouble escaping from the claws of story thinking. The right song will immediately bring you back to the here and now. Hearing the notes of the music, you will fly almost automatically towards the star of action thinking. Take a party, for instance: whether or not you get into the right mood often depends on the kind of music that's being played. Think of ways of achieving a similar effect in your everyday life. Music can have a powerful impact on your mood. It can energize you or calm you down; it's a miracle cure that we often forget to use consciously.

ACTION
Write down what kind of music tends to get you into a relaxed or creative mood. Make a playlist of these songs. Consider making a few lists for different types of feelings that you would like to evoke: confidence, energy, joy, light, courage. As soon as you notice that you would like to change your mood, select the appropriate playlist.
Put this music on for at least three minutes. Lean back and let the music wash over you. Make sure you pay attention afterwards to the effect the music has had on your mood and your working rhythm.

TRIGGER WORDS & MANTRAS

THE SECRET OF HOLLYWOOD AND TOP ATHLETES

Trigger words or mantras are brief, pointed words or sentences that immediately affect your behaviour, without all sorts of odd thoughts getting in the way. They raise your awareness and draw you into the here and now. They bring home to you, in a brief, effective way, where you want the focus of your attention to be.

This is a highly effective technique, even with an activity as linguistic or verbal as writing a screenplay. Many Hollywood screenwriters have notes propped up behind their keyboards with some short, inspiring sentence. The sentence is intended to keep their plot on track. It might be a premise like 'ambition leads to success', or the opposite, 'ambition leads to downfall'. They are short reminders that send the story in a particular direction. Similarly, trigger words or mantras can also guide our actions in a particular direction, without being attached to some whole long story that may actually hold us back from taking the necessary action.

Trigger words and 'priming'

The socio-psychologist John Bargh has researched what he calls 'automaticity': the ability to perform a task without your mind having to concern itself with all the minor details that go into it.

Other psychologists had labelled this mental process 'mindless', but Bargh has shown that it consists of unconscious or automatic processes.

An interesting part of his work was a study of 'priming', in which one group of test subjects had to perform a task involving a lot of stereotypical words for the elderly, like 'old', 'grey' and 'forgetful'. The other group were not 'primed' with these words. After performing this task, the two groups were asked to go to a different room. Strangely enough, it turned out that the first group had acquired some of the behaviour associated with the elderly: they walked much more slowly than the second group.

If you give a group of people an assignment with encouraging words ('I'm sure you can do this'), and you give a second group the same assignment with a discouraging warning ('everybody finds this very difficult'), the first group will learn faster and in a more satisfying way.

The idea behind 'priming' is that you can influence your behaviour with language. And this explains how 'trigger words' can be used. Trigger words guide behaviour in a far more effective way than long-winded instructions, because they set off automatic, unconscious processes. In the terms of our method, they help you switch from thoughts to feeling and to steer clear of the temptation of story thinking.

Trigger words and professional sport

Professional athletes constantly use trigger words. In the final of the French Open a few years ago, the tennis player Justine Henin, who was 4–1 up in the first set, took a sealed envelope out of her tennis bag and tore it open. It contained a note with the trigger words 'COURIR, COURIR, COURIR ('run, run, run') in capital letters. You might think, 'What rubbish, that's so obvious, it's ridiculous!', but Henin, who was the world number one at the time, knew that she might lose the way and tighten up. She reinvigorated herself mentally with a few simple trigger words. At 6–1, 5–2 in her favour, she opened another envelope.

Trigger words and mantras are two powerful instruments that can shift you to action thinking or help to keep you there.

Mantras

Mantras are sentences that you frequently use to conjure up the right feeling. The American life coach Anthony Robbins uses mantras in his training sessions. We find them so powerful that, with his permission, we've added them to the chapter 'The art of action': 'Every day in every way I'm feeling stronger and stronger, yes'. You might want to replace 'stronger and stronger' with 'happier and happier', 'more and more confident' or 'fitter and fitter'. The other mantra that Robbins uses is 'All I need is within me now'. And as in the case of the previous one, you might vary it to say 'All the strength I need is within me now' or 'all the joy I need is within me now'.[1]

The mantras work most powerfully if you say them out loud. Many people appear to find that difficult. If you are one of those people, you might ask yourself the following question. Have you ever said out loud 'My goodness, I can't believe how stupid I am'? People find this easy to say. It's just another mosquito that's allowed to take up all the space it wants, while the star shining in the background is played down or ignored.

ACTION FOR TRIGGER WORDS AND MANTRAS

1 Write down a trigger word and/or mantra that reminds you of your values and your purpose. Stick it on your bathroom mirror, or put it in the settings of the opening screen on your mobile phone or your computer.

2 Write down a trigger word and/or mantra that reminds you of your goals. Stick it on your bathroom mirror , or put it in the settings of the opening screen on your mobile phone or your computer.

1   Used by permission from Robbins Research International, Inc. For more information go to www.tonyrobbins.com

THE ART OF ACTION

Do you want to experience the Mindset method in a practical, tangible and compact way? In 'The art of action' you apply the pillars, the four types of concentration and the instruments in just 30 minutes. You focus on the here and now, accept the past, and create images for the future.

THE ART OF ACTION

CREATING NEW HABITS

A daily training program for action thinking

There are days that you struggle to get up in the morning. At times like that you may feel discouraged by everything that lies ahead. As soon as you wake up, your head quickly fills up with all kinds of things. The work that has to be done that day, things going on in your personal life, irritations about certain recent events and problems that have not yet been resolved. Also, you may often get the feeling that there is too little time to get everything done. Of course you are sometimes looking forward to parts of the day ahead, but even then you may find all kinds of story-thinking details creeping in. In fact it's all become a sort of daily routine: you get up, and your life is automatically surrounded by the usual veil of story thinking. Not clear and sharply defined, but a rather misty atmosphere. An irritating cloud of mosquitoes.

If you decide to break with this routine and you want to start off the day in action thinking, there's a simple way to do it. Disrupting the routine is an essential first step: decide to take twenty minutes off for a walk, preferably in a park or in natural surroundings. In total this will take at most half an hour, including getting dressed and so on. While on this walk, you keep to a number of actions.

This will ensure that you begin the day energetically, with a clear head, and in the here and now. If you think you have no time for this, it means that you are deciding not to break with your routine of story thinking. That's a choice. It's simply a question of getting up half an hour earlier, or starting later. Your day will be different. It will make a world of difference. What often stops you doing it is that you're convinced you have no time. But the whole point is that if you take half an hour a day to train action thinking, you will literally find that you gain time and perform actions with more satisfaction and focused attention. That's how you prepare for the day ahead and change your old patterns of behaviour. You release the energy that is necessary to perform actions with total concentration and to start on your day with keen anticipation. And another important thing: you won't have to force yourself to do it any more. Forcing yourself never feels good. When you use friendly eyes to guide your actions, on the other hand, you automatically feel a kind of determination taking over. The walk will help you to shift into action thinking in a natural way.

Making time for fully focused attention

Some people already do something of the kind intuitively, while they're cycling, driving, or taking the bus or train to work. Even so, this doesn't have the same kind of power and effect. It's certainly useful to practise action thinking at moments like this, but that is fundamentally different from what we propose. An essential part of our method is practising walking with self-confidence, like an athlete, and you can't do that in the car, in the train, or on a bicycle. Below we give a structured pattern of actions that will keep out distractions and provide a more concrete framework for training action thinking methodically. When you walk like an athlete, you feel your body filling with self-confidence. This will influence the quality of your thoughts. The fact that you are taking time out for yourself is crucial. Almost everyone complains of not having any time for himself or herself. That too is a choice. What stops you from taking half an hour a day off for yourself? We often hear people say it's impossible because of obligations relating to their work, children and so on. But if you were to add up all the minutes you spend every day worrying and the minutes you spend doing completely irrelevant things, you might find it comes to a lot more than half an hour. So going for a walk after you have got up and before you get down to your everyday activities works best. That you have no time to do this is simply a perception. Self-discipline is joyful anticipation. This walk is a simple way of getting a small physical workout and a perfect mental preparation for your day.

Creating passion

You can only learn to produce passion from 'feeling'. One of the key ways of doing so is the first pillar: friendly eyes. The point is to bring peace to your fretting brain and the noise in your head; otherwise it's impossible to be in the moment. By using 'friendly eyes', you can calm down the pinball machine of your thoughts and alleviate the stress in your body. Of course, thoughts will never be completely absent. Nor do they have to be. The point is that you learn to identify with thoughts that are useful. You learn to disregard all the other noise and irrelevant thoughts. In this way you reach real 'presence of mind': you're in the here and now, you're both alert and calm at the same time, you're determined. So now you're ready for action. You don't have to force anything. 'Determination' is a calm, pleasant, stress-free state. Forcing and 'musts' lead to stress and not to presence of mind. They lead to a 'malfunctioning machine', a body that is tight and rigid from stress. These two states are opposite poles. Essentially, we are far too inclined to remain stuck in thoughts instead of shifting to feeling.

The method proposed by 'Mindset in daily life' seeks to *raise consciousness*, the ultimate aim being to allow your life to be guided by the right feeling *unconsciously*. That means learning to act instinctively, on the basis of feeling. Becoming conscious of your 'feeling' will also affect the quality of your thoughts. You can experience and practice this every day by carrying out 'the art of action' regularly every morning. How satisfying it would feel to train your mindset to work from action thinking by starting off your day perfectly with twenty minutes every morning!

In applying 'the art of action', you are no longer rationalizing. You teach your brain to react both physically and mentally using action thinking. By using trigger words, consciously directing images, conjuring up friendly eyes, good mistakes, and acceptance, you will learn, one step at a time, to start your day with a different energy level. You will use visualization and replace 'thoughts' with 'feeling'. Now you'll be ready to start your day on the basis of feeling instead of thoughts.

ACTION
Once a week, perform the twenty-minute training program of 'the art of action', to start your day in action thinking.
See the program on the next page. Keep to the time limit for each element. In the six-minute element of action thinking, you will practice gratitude, forgiveness, and compassion. If necessary, look back at the assignments associated with the pillars if you are unsure of how to do this.

THE ART OF ACTION

WALK LIKE AN ATHLETE
During this walk, keep walking like an athlete for 20 minutes. Do this from the beginning to the end. Be aware of how you are moving. Your pace is faster than usual. You feel strong and confident. Your posture is straight, your shoulders relaxed. You take firm steps.

SCAN AND ZOOM
Look around you and scan your surroundings. What can you see that you have never noticed before? Zoom in on details, experience their beauty. Listen to a sound you like: the wind, a bird, the rustling of leaves. Enjoy and be thankful for what you see and hear.

1 min.

MANTRA – Say out loud:
All I need is within me now.

You can add words, like: '*All the joy I need is within me now*.' Keep walking like an athlete, feel your body.

1 min.

BREATHING AND TAPPING
Inhale strongly 4 times through your nose, then exhale strongly 4 times through your mouth. Tap the tops of your fingers in time with your breathing. First thumb to index finger, then thumb to middle finger, then thumb to ring finger, then thumb to little finger (use only the right hand).

2 min.

ACTION THINKING
> **GRATITUDE** Friendly eyes
> **FORGIVENESS** Good mistakes
> **COMPASSION** Acceptance

6 min.

VISUALIZE TODAY
Visualize 3 actions for today, schedule them and commit to them:
- One action for yourself
- One action for your work
- One action for those you love

Make sure the actions are linked to your values and goals.

3 min.

MANTRA – Say out loud:
Every day in every way, I'm feeling stronger and stronger. Yes.

You can alternate the word '*stronger*' with words like '*happier*' or '*healthier*.'

1 min.

VISUALIZE THE FUTURE
See before you that you've achieved something that hasn't happened yet. Feel the pleasure of this achievement, the smiles, the laughter, the people around you, the result. Be specific: where are you? Who is around you? What have you achieved? How does that feel?

5 min.

DELIGHT IN YOUR DAY
Finish your walk with steady, confident steps. Scan and zoom, look around you. Be grateful for this moment. What are you looking forward to today? What do the actions look like? To whom will they bring pleasure? How will they react? You're now ready for the day, delight in it.

1 min.

CREATING PASSION

POETRY

This book has set out to show that we all tend to be too absorbed in 'thoughts' and that we could benefit from living more on the basis of 'feeling'. All day long, stories are going through our heads. Our days are full of reasoning and conclusions, rationalizations, trains of thought and arguments. Spiritual thinkers like Eckhart Tolle say that we are selling ourselves short by primarily valuing the rational and verbal sides of our nature, and urge us to strive to reconnect with a deeper source of life. We might experience this, for instance, by looking at a flower or a bird. Not in the way that a florist or ornithologist might look, but with an open, non-analytical gaze. Tolle calls birds and flowers 'messengers from another realm', whose beauty can help us to reconnect with our deepest, true nature. We might be able to struggle free from the ego that wants to label everything around us and capture it in a rational context. It's a process sometimes described as 'experiencing the Essence of things'.

Poets seek to do something similar. They try to recapture what we've lost in language by turning it into a mere instrument that helps us control the world – its playful, magical, original qualities – by allowing language to speak for itself. Sometimes by disrupting it, sometimes by reaffirming its affinity with music, sometimes by giving it back its numinous quality. In short: by invoking

the voice it once possessed, which has become weakened over the course of time.

For most of us, literary poetry is 'out of our comfort zone', because it often seems hard to understand. But that's precisely where the magic begins. So we thought it fitting to finish this book not with a resounding conclusion, but with a poem.

Hans' personal tip to you, the reader, is 'let go'.
Just read the words, it doesn't matter if you don't totally understand the poem. This is a great finishing moment for 'feeling instead of thought'.

Even in this place at the edge of civilization
the unassailable stands out like a rough wheel-rim.
Even this place can't be conceived without the life
that defines itself in formulas.
The constant curbs of precepts,
the untold boundaries, the nodding words.
Yet the unperformed and untouched are there too,
whose bodies can't be captured by their shapes,
nor in their ethereal nakedness.
And here and there is light without a shadow.

Hans Dekkers

ACKNOWLEDGMENTS

We want to thank a great many people for the enormous amount of support we've received over the past years since '*Mindset a mental guide for sport*' was first launched in 2007. It seems as if that first book launch happened yesterday, and we can say without a doubt that since Mindset has 'been there', we have both been able to enjoy the 'now' more than before. The people we've been privileged to meet along the way, in all the Mindset training courses and trips we've undertaken, have made it all worthwhile and enriched our lives, as we hope we have enriched theirs.

Jackie about Hans
Hans, no words are enough: your fantastic sense of humour, your perseverance and your amazing way with words. Also the fact that you agreed to the proposal of shutting ourselves away for a week together in Lisbon to get our second darling finished once and for all, was extremely brave of you!

Hans about Jackie
Jackie, you are the driving force behind this book, which would never have come into existence without your inspiration, patience, humour, and your big, generous heart. Thanks for everything. But please, no more horrible instant coffee!

Hans: I want to thank Stasja for her involvement and loyalty while we were writing this book. The fact that she carried on thinking and reading with me undoubtedly helped keep me on track and grounded. Without her support and analytical mind, there would have been no *Mindset in daily life*.

Jackie: My wonderful partner Jacqueline van Meyel – Jacko. Her love and insight keep me balanced! Without her support, her knowledge and her contribution, Mindset would probably have vanished into the cloud of mosquitoes. Her feedback on both the books and the trainings is highly valued. I'm grateful to her, appreciative of everything she has done.

My Dutch family, the 'Van Meyels', have been of tremendous support over the years. Always knowing that I am welcome and feeling the safety and kindness of a warm family has to be one of the best things that has happened to me.

We received indispensable and inspiring feedback from Nora Blom and Annette Veth. They patiently read the content of our book and supported us along the way. This gave us courage and confidence. We appreciate them both as kind and wise friends. Special friends that have stood by us for years and freely shared their knowledge with us are: Ay Mey Lie, Alberto ter Doest, Jan Moors, Sandra Landa, Ellen van Doorne and Ineke Kraus.

Thanks also go to our graphic designer Aart Jan Bergshoeff. His creativity has helped us develop the Mindmaps, and with his many other talents he has helped to keep everything on track.

The Mindset training sessions we conducted in South Africa brought us into contact with Sampie Pienaar, a remarkable entrepreneur. After reading our first book and following the training sessions, Sampie invited us to implement Mindset in his companies. His insights, patience and cheerfulness, helped to raise our game and also was a part of the inspiration to write this book.

For 'The art of action' we were given permission to use Anthony Robbins's breathing exercise and mantras.
Used by permission of Robbins Research International, Inc.
For more information, please go to www.tonyrobbins.com

This book is dedicated to two of Jackie and Jacko's soulmates, Ellen Baarslag and Sandra Polderman. They were killed in January 2012, while cycling around Argentina on their tandem. When El and San came into a room, it lit up. They were two pure action thinkers. We shall never stop missing them. Silence is love.

RECOMMENDED READING

FRIENDLY EYES

Marshall B. Rodenburg: *Non-Violent Communication: A Language of life.* PuddleDancer Press. California, USA 2003.

GOOD MISTAKES

Brené Brown: *The Gifts of Imperfection.* Hazelden Publishing. Minnesota, USA 2010.

CURIOSITY

Adam Kahane: *Power and Love: A Theory and Practice of Social Change.* Berrett-Koehler Publishers. San Francisco, USA 2010.

SELF-KNOWLEDGE

Stephen R. Covey: *The Seven Habits of Highly Effective People.* Simon & Schuster. New York, USA 1989.

SELF-DISCIPLINE

Stephen M.R. Covey: *The Speed of Trust.* Simon and Schuster. UK 2006.

ACCEPTANCE

William Hart: *The Art of Living.* Harper. San Francisco, USA 1987.

CONCENTRATION

Jim Loehr and Tony Schwartz: *The Power of Full Engagement.* Free Press Paperbacks. New York, USA 2003.

Robert M. Nideffer: *Attention control training.* Wyden Books, New York USA 1976.

FEELING INSTEAD OF THOUGHT

Jill Bolte Taylor: *My Stroke of Insight: A Brain Scientist's Personal Journey.* Viking Penguin. USA 2008.

Eckhart Tolle: *The Power of Now.* New World Library. USA, 1999.

Eckhart Tolle: *A New Earth: Awakening to Your Life's Purpose.* Dutton, USA 2005.

VISUALIZATION

Amy L.Baltzell: *Living in the Sweet Spot. Preparing for performance in Sport and life*. Fitness Information Technology. West Virginia University, USA 2011.

MEDITATION

The work of S.N. Goenka: www.dhamma.org

Joseph Goldstein: *Insight Meditation*. Shambhala Publications, Inc. Boston, Massachusetts, USA 1993.

Andy Puddicombe: *Get some Headspace*. Hodder & Stoughton General Division, UK 2012.

BREATHING

Andrew Weil: *Breathing: The Master Key to Self-Healing*. Audio Book. USA 2006.

YOGA

B.K.S. Iyengar: *Light on Yoga*. Schocken Books. New York, USA 1966.

NATURE

Alan Jacobs, Thoreau: *Transcendent Nature for a Modern World*. Watkins Publishing, UK 2012.

TRIGGER WORDS & MANTRAS

Daniel Kahneman: *Thinking Fast and Slow*. Farrar, Strauss and Giroux, New York, USA 2011.

MISCELLANEOUS

Don Miguel Ruiz: *The Four Agreements*. Amber-Allen Publishing/ California, USA, 2007.

Chade-Meng Tan: *Search Inside Yourself*. HarperCollins Publishers. London, UK, 2012.

Daniel Goleman: *Working with Emotional Intelligence*. Bloomsbury Publishing, London, UK 1998.

Jackie Reardon and Hans Dekkers: *Personal Success Plan for Action Thinking*. Mindset Publishers. Amsterdam, Netherlands 2008.

Jackie Reardon and Hans Dekkers: *Mindset*. Mindset Publishers. Amsterdam, Netherlands 2007.

Made in the USA
Columbia, SC
14 July 2021

41842259R00104